Blessings!

John Gillespie

The Power of Seven Personal Financial Disciplines

How to Grow & Preserve Your Estate
& Avoid the Next Market Meltdown

Title ID: 4450606
ISBN-13: 978-0615891934
Copyright © 2013
John G. Gillespie

By
John G. Gillespie, CEP, RFC

Published by
BeyondYourManuscript.com

Words on John Gillespie

There is something that I have found to be a common element amongst the successful professionals that I have worked with over the past 17 years. It's an element I've found in accountants, bankers, attorneys and other financial advisers which I think distinguishes the mere dilettante from the true professional, and that is character. I think a true "professional" is someone who is willing to take his client's problems and make them his own. After all, one will work hardest to solve his own problems over most any others, right?

John Gillespie has that critical element of character, and he is one whom I would deem to be a true professional. His skill and expertise have benefited my clients on many occasions. His advice and counsel has solved many of their problems, or, even better, helped avoid those problems from ever arising at all. Few people that I've worked with have exhibited such a high degree of character. Even fewer, in my definition, are true professionals. John is such in every sense of the word.

You are most fortunate to hold in your hand a valuable resource for yourself and your family. This book will provide many great benefits, both in substantive knowledge, and in life-enriching guidance. It will do so because it was written by a man of character, a man who is willing to take your problems and make them his own.

L. David McBride, Attorney-at-Law
September 2013

"The strategies and disciplines within this book have guided our advisors and their clients to greater success. These principles will revolutionize an individual's estate and investment outlook."

Malachi P. Sturlin, CFP, RFC,
Senior Vice President,
Access Financial Group, Inc.

"John Gillespie has done something quite remarkable – combined humor, deep faith, and solid financial advice...all in one book. You will find wisdom for the basic decisions that we all need to make today in service of tomorrow."

Dan Boone, President
Travecca Nazarene University

"John Gillespie's life purpose (see page 150) reflects who he is and how he relates to people. This book is credible, informed and helpful."

Dr. Lyle B. Pointer,
Church of the Nazarene,
Mount Vernon, Washington

Contents

The Early Days

Is Your Financial House in Order?

Blissful Ignorance is Not Blissful

The Tragedy of Tradition

Mr. Macho is Sleeping with Mrs. Ignorance

Breaking the Family Generational Curse of Financial Illiteracy

The Data Gathering Process – Starting at the Starting Point

Your Personalized Financial Plan

Where There is a Will, There May Still be a Mess

Living Probate

Death Probate

Six Easy Steps to a Complete Estate Plan

What Your Executor/Successor Trustee Needs to Know

The Protective Component

My First Risk Management Encounter

A Financial and Spiritual Encounter

Do You Really Need It?

What is the Right Amount of Coverage?

Types of Life Insurance

How to Protect Your Investment Portfolio

You Can Spend it All

The Three Greatest Financial Problems in the World

Record Keeping

Your Emergency Fund

The Rule of 72

Retirement or Re-Engagement?

Wealth Building: The Accumulation Phase

Pay Yourself First

Dollar Cost Averaging

Should I Contribute to My 401(k) Plan?

Living Off Your Nest Egg: The Income Phase

Honey, I'm Home Forever

Getting All the Life You Can out of the Money You Have

We are Going to Travel When the Dog Dies

Foreword

You have the power to change your life. Power is not only the ability to act, it is also the ability to produce an effect. Occasionally, a leader comes along with a vision that enables him to equip others to release the power that is within them. That leader, however, must have done it first. He has to lead from the front. He has to have withstood the testing that only time can bring. He has to have emerged from life's daily battles more determined when defeated, and humble when victorious. In order to not become enslaved to tradition, there may be times he has to bravely venture into the unknown. Even when so-called industry experts claim that what you are attempting to do cannot be done, a leader finds a better way and moves forward. A leader has the ability to shut out his industry's noise. He pursues the betterment of everyone around him. That is the kind of leader that authored *The Power of Seven Personal Financial Disciplines.*

Leading in the capacity of senior pastor and enjoying the blessing of serving one of America's mega-churches keeps you continuously alert as to who you can trust with the daily issues that require utmost confidentiality. Over the years I have adhered to the practice of maintaining three key financial consultants in my life. I have worked with a CPA firm to handle tax filings, an attorney to handle legal matters, and an investment advisor for investment decisions. My personal life language profile causes me to believe strongly in "making a plan and working your plan". From my very first initial meeting with John Gillespie, he laid out a plan and cast the vision of what the future could hold financially. Since that day, back in the early 2000's, I chose to move forward with the execution of that plan. I have witnessed the faithfulness and integrity with which he works. John Gillespie loves God, his wife (to whom he has been married 37 years), his children, and his grandchildren. I have seen his work firsthand as I have flown around the Midwest with him in his private plane. As his pastor, I can simply say he is the real deal. He lives what he teaches. Investors, advisors, corporations, and multiple mega-ministries, which his conglomerate of companies serves, place their confidence in him daily.

Stewardship requires planning. A steward is one who manages another's property or finances. *The Power of Seven Personal Financial Disciplines* lays out a plan for you and your advisors as you attempt to manage the resources that have been entrusted to you. The number *seven* is synonymous with refinement and perfection. God took seven days to create the earth. I believe the seven personal financial disciplines that are spelled out in this book can bring refinement and a new dimension of clarity and confidence into your life as you face your financial future.

A discipline is an activity that develops or improves a skill. An adherence to certain disciplines will eventually bring a desired result. I believe that as you read this book you, like me, will be the blessed benefactor of *The Power of Seven Personal Financial Disciplines*.

Mark Crow,
husband, father, pastor, author & leader
VictoryChurch.tv

Introduction

"Sometimes in life you just do what you have to do. When times are tough, it makes you tough." ---John Gillespie

Some people will undoubtedly struggle over the word "discipline" in the title of this book. I know the word discipline is not exactly PC (politically correct) these days. If you are reading this book, then you are not afraid of the word discipline. Discipline is not used here as an imposed restriction and most definitely not as a punishment to enhance behavior. Discipline is a high character quality and a systematic instruction intended for training in a craft or trade. These disciplines will be wealth building and financial preservation principles.

The Early Days

The year was 1955. The USS Nautilus, the first nuclear-powered submarine, was sent out to sea for the first time. The Pentagon announced plans to develop ICBMs (intercontinental ballistic missiles). Dwight D. Eisenhower was president. Ray Kroc opened his first McDonald's. Disneyland opened to the public. Actor James Dean was killed in an automobile accident at age 24. The Mickey Mouse Club made its debut. The first footage of Elvis Presley was filmed. General Motors Corporation became the first American Corporation to make a profit of over $1 billion in one year. Steve Jobs was born in California and proceeded to innovate his way into technological stardom.

Each of the above incidences proved to be historically significant. However, there were two African American women that challenged tradition in 1955 and changed the course of history. On March 2, Claudette Colvin, a 15-year-old girl, refused to give up her seat on a bus in Montgomery, Alabama to a white woman after the driver demanded she do so. She was carried off the bus backwards and was kicked, handcuffed and harassed on the way to the police station. In that same city on December 1, Rosa Parks refused to obey bus driver James F. Blake's order that she give up her seat to make room for a white passenger. Her arrest led to the Montgomery bus boycott. These two ladies had such a powerful, positive impact on the ongoing social structure of this nation that each of their legacies will live on forever. We will discover later in this book that legacy is so much more than the eventual distribution of financial wealth.

I was born in 1955 in the "one-traffic-light" town of Adrian, Georgia. I often tell people that I came from a talking family. Daddy was a preacher, and Mama was, well, she was a woman. (That was a joke – a bad joke, but a joke nonetheless.) As denominational pastors will do, Daddy pastored several Nazarene churches over a 60-year span. Mama served as an LPN (licensed practical nurse) in order to help keep food on the table.

I believe values are caught, not taught. I feel blessed beyond belief to have caught my parents' values and to know that my children caught mine.

Early in my childhood, we moved to Barnesville, Georgia. Money was really tight. Mama had an old car, and every time she turned left, the horn would blow and the passenger door would swing open and then back shut. These were the fun days before seatbelts. My sisters and I would hang over the passenger door so that every time mom turned left, we would ride the door out and ride it back in. In order to get back home after we had gone into downtown Barnesville, we would have to turn left in front of the police station on Atlanta Street. Sure enough, Mom would turn left, the horn would blow, the policeman would wave, we would ride that door out, and then it would swing shut and deposit us safely back into the car.. Now that was fun. Just think, my mama would be arrested if that happened today. Oh well, I guess Dad could fulfill his ministerial duties and then go visit her in jail. My parents always taught us to look at the bright side of life. We were broke, but never knew it. We were broke, but never poor. As a child I remember that once a week Dad would say to Mom, "Honey, get the checkbook, and let's try to pay some bills". Sometimes those sessions ended with my mom in tears. Something would stir inside my young heart, saying, "Someday things are going to get better." I witnessed a supernatural faith in my parents. They told me that

God would always provide, and He did! I grew up in a home that was in top shape spiritually, but like many, we struggled to keep our financial house in order.

Dad pastored churches in Columbus, Georgia during my junior high years and in Augusta, Georgia during my high school years. While in high school, I worked as an apprentice for a wallpaper hanger and learned the trade. I remember early on grasping the knowledge that, with a skilled trade, I would never go hungry. If I was willing to work, there would always be work. I did not realize it at the time, but that skill would financially enable me to work my way through Trevecca Nazarene University in Nashville, Tennessee. Thanks to Harold Latham in the public relations department, I traveled with the college quartet on weekends, which also helped to cover my tuition. My wife and I met at the University and married in 1975. I was a junior pursuing a music education major, and she was a senior completing an accounting major. She eventually graduated summa cum laude, and I eventually graduated praise the laude. We look back on those years and wonder how we ever made it financially. To this day she still brags about how she could make four meals for the two of us out of one chicken. Sometimes in life you just do what you have to do. When times are tough, it makes you tough.

On the weekends and Wednesdays, I served as a praise and worship pastor for area churches, and my wife accompanied me on the piano. Over the years we have been honored to lead music ministries in Nashville, TN at Inglewood, Donelson, and Bethel Nazarene; in Memphis, TN at Grace Nazarene; and in Oklahoma City, OK at Western Oaks, Calvary and in the early 2000's led the contemporary service at Bethany First Nazarene. I have always believed that music helps to move the soul.

My degree in music education launched my extensive and grueling career in public education. I taught school for four long months. I filled in the last half of the year for a lady on maternity leave at Antioch High School in Nashville, Tennessee. I have never been so glad to see a baby come in all my life. My love and admiration for our educators deepened immensely. I was like a duck out of water. My tolerance of bad attitudes is extremely low. I thought that, like me, everybody jumped out of bed every morning excited and ready to conquer the world. Boy, was I wrong. You know something is not right when you roll over in bed in the morning, refusing to go to school but then realizing you are the teacher. I had diarrhea for four months. Listen to your digestive system. It can help guide your life. If it is making crude noises that it should not make, then it may be trying to tell you something.

In 1978 an older gentleman at the church in which I was serving as the praise and worship pastor approached me and said, "If you ever need a job, come and see me." My wife headed up the investigation into what he may be offering, and we soon discovered that he sold subterranean real estate. That's a nice way of saying he sold cemetery property. Since my appetite had begun to outgrow the 1/8 of a chicken I had for dinner, I decided to apply for work. Joe Tinnell employed me through Service Corporation International (SCI) as a prearrangement burial counselor at Hermitage Memorial Gardens in Hermitage, a suburb of Nashville, Tennessee. I did the only thing any respectable 23-year-old should do that had accepted that job. I bought my wife and myself two cemetery lots. You can imagine how that excited her beyond belief. Well, the beyond belief part was accurate. I would not exactly say she was excited. I knew I had messed up when dinner deteriorated to Vienna sausage and boiled peanuts. Have you ever examined the contents listed on a can of Red Bird Vienna sausage? I'm talking about pork spleen, pork stomach and anything else they can scrape off the sausage floor. To make things worse, she would ask me every night when I got home whether or not I had sold anything. I finally said, "Look, if I ever do sell anything, I'll tell you, so just stop asking." After six weeks, with absolutely zero results, I finally said, "If I don't sell anything this week, I guess I'll have to go try something else." I felt like I could dangle my legs off of a dime. *I have never forgotten that darkness before dawn moment.* Old Joe wanted me to win as badly as I did, but he knew there was really nothing he could do.

I knew Joe was a praying man. He stopped me as I was walking down the stairs the next day, put his hand on my shoulder and said, "Son, the Good Book promises, 'I will never leave you or forsake you.'" Within the next couple of days, business started flowing, and it never stopped. I was soon promoted to Family Service Director and eventually into management.

SCI transferred me from Nashville to Memphis, Tennessee to manage Memphis Memory Gardens. Part of the Family Service Director's responsibility was to greet the processionals at the gate of the cemetery and lead them to the graveside. One day we had two funerals scheduled to take place at approximately the same time. As I sat at the gate in my 1973 beige Datsun pickup truck, I noticed that both flower trucks had already entered the park. I then saw the police motorcycle flashing lights and realized that both processionals were approaching the cemetery from opposite directions at exactly the same time. A young groundsman came running up to my truck and said, "Mr. Gillespie, we've got a problem. The flower trucks got mixed up, and they have put the flowers on the wrong graves." I calmly said, "Well, don't worry about it. I am sure they will never notice. When the services end, we will get the flowers switched back correctly." I led the first processional to its graveside, opened the door of the family car and escorted a nice little lady to the tent for her husband's burial. When we arrived at the tent, she stopped in her tracks. There was a huge streamer hanging off of a large arrangement of flowers that said, "BIG MAMA." She asked loudly, "Who is Big Mama?" I quickly confessed our sin. Upon the conclusion of the service, the trucks immediately made a mad dash and reversed their mistake. I served for 18 months in Memphis before SCI transferred me to Oklahoma City, Oklahoma to Resthaven Memory Gardens. Those 5 1/2 years in the cemetery industry were filled with a lot of fun memories. Above all else, it gave me a healthy perspective as to how amazingly limited our time on this earth is. I was continuously amazed at the number of young people we buried.

I was looking for an off-ramp from all the transfers that came with corporate life. In 1982, the year I arrived in Oklahoma City, a friend introduced me to the financial services industry. Having served those years in the cemetery industry, I was just excited about being among the living. I will explain more as to the circumstances that brought me into the financial industry in Chapter 3. For now let's start examining some financial matters.

Is Your Financial House in Order?

It is easy to live with a false sense of security that your financial house is "in order." However, sometimes things are not as they appear. Take the 100-mile-an-hour goat for instance. Two guys are hunting in the woods when they come across a clearing and a really deep hole. In fact, the hole is so deep that they can't see the bottom. One man says to the other, "Let's get something and throw it down the hole to see how long it takes to hit bottom." They scurry around to find something, but all they can find is an old automobile transmission. They carry the transmission to the hole and toss it in. Almost immediately, they hear a rustling in the bushes and look up to see a goat running straight at them, doing about 100 miles an hour. They both step aside, and the goat jumps head first down the hole. A farmer appears from the other side of the clearing and says, "Hey, have you guys seen my goat?" "As a matter of fact, we have," responds one of the men. "Your goat came out of the bushes, running straight at us and jumped into that big hole." The farmer replies, "Oh, that couldn't have been my goat". "I had my goat chained to an automobile transmission."

Like those hunters, sometimes our actions can have unintended consequences. It is important to know what the potential consequences can be from a financial action plan. If you have no comprehensive financial plan, you face a future of uncertainty, potential financial devastation and possibly even unnecessary litigation. Having no plan can lead to a deep hole that seems to have no bottom. My intention in writing this book is to equip you with the necessary information so that, along with your professional advisors, you can arrive at a well-defined, all-encompassing, comprehensive plan to accomplish your financial goals.

A financial action plan to *"get your financial house in order"* should include consideration of the seven following financial disciplines: Comprehensive Financial Awareness, Estate Planning, Risk Management, Cash Management, Retirement Planning, Tax Strategies and Asset Allocation. Each discipline requires answers to certain questions that only you can answer. Let's examine some of those questions.

Comprehensive Financial Awareness sets the stage for successful financial outcomes. A comprehensive data-gathering process reveals the questions that need to be answered to determine where you currently are financially and where you need to be in the days ahead. You might be thinking "why all the personal questions?" Well, imagine your physician walking into your exam room and offering a diagnosis and prescribing a treatment without any form of examination. That would be ridiculous. I have met people who have accepted financial prescriptions without proper examination.

Estate Planning requires you to answer the following questions: What do I have? Where do I want it to go? How do I want my heirs to receive distributions, lump sum or on-going income? Who do I want to serve as my successor trustee, executor, POA power of attorney for financial matters and health care matters? Do I want to spare my heirs the hassle and expense of probate? If my beneficiaries were to predecease me, where would I want their share of the estate to go? Do I want to include my church or charity in the distribution of my assets?

Risk Management addresses these issues: How will my spouse and dependent heirs survive financially in the event of my premature death? Am I properly protected if faced with catastrophic illness, disability, long-term care, and property and casualty loss?

Cash Management looks at the challenge of maintaining a properly funded emergency fund. Do I have 3 to 6 months of my living expenses set aside as readily available resources, with checkbook access, for all of life's little emergencies? Am I maintaining good records and receipts for accounting purposes?

Retirement Planning reveals the importance of having a nest egg that will fund my eventual "non-income earning" years. If I am still in my pre-retirement years, what target amount of money must be attained in order to maintain my current standard of living throughout retirement? Once that is determined, then I need to know how that goal translates into a monthly accumulation amount that will fulfill the retirement goal. If I am in retirement, what distribution amount could I withdraw periodically, if necessary, without prematurely exhausting the principal throughout my lifetime? What rates of return will be required to accomplish all of this?

Tax Strategies can help you reap net benefits to your annual revenue, total net worth, and even gross estate distribution. What strategies could lower my current taxable income? Could I benefit from financial tools that generate tax deductions, tax deferred accumulation and tax free distributions? With the current complexity of the tax code, is my reluctance to hire a professional actually costing me more than I realize?

Asset Allocation is the selective placement of your investable resources into goal-focused investments. To assist you in your selections and tailor your investment vehicles around your objectives, your advisor should help you with certain questions. What is my risk tolerance, investment objectives and time horizon? Do I want to utilize an active management strategy that will move my funds into the market and then back to safer havens from time to time,or, do I want a traditional static buy and hold strategy? Since the market meltdowns in recent years, that approach is often referred to as "buy and hope." In light of the fact that some major indices can be extremely volatile, maybe you should not only ask about the buy discipline of the plan but about the sell discipline as well.

Certain major transitional events in life, like kindergarten, college, graduation, marriage, having children, job transitions and retirement, can often bring an acute awareness of how well we have planned. After one man retired and sat around the house a while, his wife said to me, "Help! My husband has just retired and doesn't know what to do with himself." She continued, "I just realized I now have twice the husband and half the money." Evidently, she was questioning the trade-off.

Now that you know the questions, we will begin the process of helping you find the answers to each of them. Getting one's financial house in order starts from wherever you are today. Create a plan and work your plan. Revisit these questions occasionally in light of your goals. And be careful about throwing things into dark holes.

Chapter One

Discipline One: Comprehensive Financial Awareness

"Money is nothing more than a utility that allows us to get all that we possibly can out of life." ---John Gillespie

Blissful Ignorance Is Not Blissful

Do you know where you are financially? If you feel clueless regarding a personal comprehensive financial awareness, then welcome to the human race. The majority of the people in this world are so immersed in the daily grind of attempting to reposition the world's wealth that they have not even taken the time to assess their personal financial status. The very thought of comparing their current status to where they should be at this point in the journey frightens them immensely. If you do not have a healthy comprehensive view of your financial status, then there is no way to know how well or how poorly you are doing in moving toward a reasonable financial goal. If you are doing well, you will surely want to know that you are on track with your accomplishments. However, if you are off track, even in the slightest, why would you ever think that ignoring it would make it better? You do realize that close only counts in horseshoes and hand grenades, right? As a private pilot, when I depart Wiley Post Airport in Oklahoma City, if I am 10 degrees off course, it is not such a big deal if I am only going 100 miles to Oklahoma's Lake Eufaula. But, if I am flying to see my parents, who are 715 nautical miles away in Albany, Georgia, that 10 degrees off course from my origin might put me over the Gulf of Mexico instead of my destination. If you are ever so slightly off track in your financial accumulations now, imagine how far you might miss the mark by the time you MUST start the needed retirement income stream on which you will someday live. If you are seriously thinking "I would rather remain blissfully ignorant," then close the book now because after 31 years of successfully helping other people retire, I can assure you that blissful ignorance is not blissful, and intentional financial independence is always intentional.

The Tragedy of Tradition

Blissful ignorance can also hold us in bondage to tradition. The tragedy of tradition is the psychological enslavement to the same mindset of our predecessors. Now before you throw the baby out with the bathwater, that previous sentence does not mean that everything you have learned is wrong. The beauty of tradition is the pure joy and stability of beliefs and behaviors passed down to us from our predecessors. Hopefully, you have attained and absorbed a set of healthy core values that have enabled you to become the vibrant and effective person you are today. With all due respect and with a sincere heart of gratitude and honor to those who raised us and educated us, financial concepts and the management principles of personal finance are often horribly neglected. Families, and even educators, do their best to pass on what they know. Most often, they were never taught these financial disciplines themselves.

A refusal to break free from tradition and the psychological enslavement to the same mindset of our predecessors can financially restrict our personal development, our education, our chosen profession and our selected standard of living. In actuality, it even affects our physical and spiritual makeup – but this is a financial book, so let's proceed. *Money is nothing more than a utility that allows us to get all that we possibly can out of life.* Therefore, learning to make it, save it, accumulate it, live on it and give it might require breaking free from traditional thinking. Notice that I did not say hoard it or worship it. If you are hoarding money, you will never have enough. In fact, hoarders have even been known to face financial emergencies and borrow money rather than spend their hoarded funds. If you are worshipping money, the same emptiness that you felt even after you added onto the garage and filled it with lavish expenditures will persist. There is absolutely nothing wrong with having material abundance. The key is to fully recognize that external assets will never bring inner contentment. Money makes an awesome servant but a lousy god.

Getting all the life you can from the money you have will always bring you to acknowledge your impact in the lives of others. It really is true that no man is an island. You cannot expect to amass a fortune, insulate yourself from all other human exposure and live life with exciting purpose and personal fulfillment. How big of an impact do you really want to make?

Mr. Macho Is Sleeping with Mrs. Ignorance.

Attaining a comprehensive financial awareness brings up a critically important question. How well does your spouse understand your estate and financial plan? Was your spouse hoping to just remain blissfully ignorant, or are you bringing him or her along in the financial awareness journey? Does your spouse express any interest in the family financial affairs, or have you chosen to dominate this area by playing Mr. Macho and sleeping with Mrs. Ignorance. For some families I have counseled through the years, that statement is exactly backward. Those couples are playing Mrs. Macho and Mr. Ignorance. Whatever the case may be, you must refuse to leave your spouse behind. Ask yourself, "How well could they manage financial issues without me?" If the answer to that question is not very pleasant, then today you must start to gradually include them in little areas where they can gain a basic understanding. It will take a lot of love, gentleness and patience, but it can be done. It is important to learn the basics of managing finances.

Statistically, women will typically outlive their husbands. I have counseled many more widows through this transition than widowers. The two statements that I hear most often are "I feel so alone" and "I feel so financially helpless." Make a habit of including your spouse in all of the financial dealings in which they are willing to participate. Equip them with a basic financial understanding in order to enable them to manage on their own, if or when it would become necessary. It is the loving thing to do.

Breaking the Family Generational Curse of Financial Illiteracy

The United States, as the forerunner in capitalism, is now reaping the benefits of a phenomenal explosion in global technology. Wise up! There will be no mercy for the financially illiterate in the future. Moving forward, individuals must commit to educate themselves and their families in the financial arena or risk falling behind. Just because you were not taught finances in school, does not give you an excuse to continue living in, or allowing your children to live in, financial ignorance. I did not say "stupidity;" I said "ignorance." A stupid person knows what to do and refuses to do it. An ignorant person does not know what to do. Massive amounts of financial data are now available everywhere you turn – the Internet, webinars, e-books and even good old-fashioned printed books that you can easily stack on the tank of the toilet. So make your resolve and repeat after me: "Financial illiteracy stops with me."

Our U.S. national debt is now in the multiplied trillions of dollars. Our government's financial obligation per American family is in the hundreds of thousands of dollars. However, the U.S. Debt Clock is increasing so rapidly that you will need to reference it often to get a feel for its enormity. Our children will ultimately bear the burden of this atrocious commitment. They must learn about money and finances NOW. They need to learn and apply three financial fundamentals: generate their own independent income; understand the dangers of debt; and know how to execute a plan to make money grow. If our children grasp these basics of finances, maintain a winning attitude, mold a plan and work that plan, prosperity will abound. This nation is exceptionally resilient, and our people are incredibly innovative.

First, generating an independent income comes only through a strong determination to become financially self-sufficient and a relentless will to win. *In order to be productive and win in your personal finances, you must understand that prosperity is not an entitlement.* You must resist the entitlement mentality that so many have allowed to poison their prospects of a better future. Often, people think they are entitled to money and wealth. No, you must earn it. Tragically, the government compounds the problem by calling welfare programs "entitlements." You must determine where you are going and not expect or allow the government to do it for you. Think about this: The more someone or some entity, like the government, gives you, the more dependent you become on them. You can eventually wake up and find yourself in bondage to the giver if you are a taker.

Rise up! *The world makes way for those who know where they are going.* Recently, I was in New York City, lower Manhattan in Times Square. Unlike Oklahoma, my home state, Times Square is, without a doubt, one of the busiest places I visit. Oklahoma is so flat and so spacious that you can literally watch your dog run away for three days. At one point while in New York, I decided to rush through the crowd as fast as I humanly could, swinging my arms, staying completely focused on my goal, a building, two blocks ahead. It is amazing what happened. The crowd parted as though they knew I knew where I was going and realized I must urgently need to get there. Little did they know that my wife had accidently left her iPhone in the ladies restroom and had sent me to recover it. All they knew was that I knew where I was going and that they needed to step aside. The world makes way for those who know where they are going. By the way, the world is still full of good, honest people, and the lost cell phone was residing safely in the hands of the courteous building security guard upon my arrival.

Second, our children need to realize how important it is to *get out and stay out of debt.* The abuse of credit can have devastating consequences. This snowball of bondage innocently begins, but it can rapidly begin to choke out songs of joy with grumblings like "I owe, I owe, so off to work I go." We will address this in Chapter 4.

Take a look at how costly it can be to borrow money. A-30 year mortgage of $150,000 at 7% would cost a total of $434,501 over the life of the loan. In addition to the $150,000 for the house, you will also pay another $284,501 to the mortgage company in interest charges. I know, I know, it is an appreciating asset. Well, it may be, if the timing of the purchase, the location and the age demographics of your city are right. But do not let this low interest rate environment lure you deeper into debt. At times, I can't help but wonder who is coming along behind all of us baby boomers that can really afford all of our indulgences.

Third, we want the kids to know how to *execute a plan to make money grow*. That plan will never be a straight shot to the top. There will be good years and bad. Even the best financial plans need to allow for some volatility. Did you ever think we would see interest rates swing to historic lows? One of the fundamentals of finance is understanding the power of compound interest. Get an 18-year-old to save $100 per month, for example, at 10% annual interest, and by age 65, he will have $1,281,919. If that same teenager waits until he is

25-years-old to begin saving this way, he will have $632,407 by age 65. If he waits until age 35 to start, he will only gain a nominal $226,048 when he is 65. At 45- he would build only $75,936 by age 65. At 55 years old, he would have accumulated just $20,484. Compounding takes time. The reason there is such a huge difference in the 18-year-old and the 25-year-old is not because of the seven year difference but rather because the 25-year-old lost 47 years of compounding on those years of contribution. Those lost years can never be recovered. The clock is ticking. The sooner your kids execute a plan, the sooner their life's goals can be fulfilled – the sooner they will be off your payroll.

Cultivate and encourage financial literacy within your own household. When it comes to becoming financially competent, tell your spouse and even your children, "We can do this." Applying all of these financial disciplines will place you well on your way to breaking any family generational curse of financial illiteracy. The world truly makes way for those who know where they are going.

The Data Gathering Process - Starting at the Starting Place

In the Introduction, I referenced how ridiculous it would be for a physician to offer a diagnosis and a prescription to a patient without a proper examination.

In order to start at the starting place, you have to initially gather the financial data that will be needed for an adviser to conduct and prepare for you an appropriate financial plan. There is not one specific format that must be followed. The key is to compile as much comprehensive data as possible and attempt to leave no stone unturned.

I have included a typical FINANCIAL AND ESTATE PLANNING INFORMATION FORM for your convenience. This is an example of the necessary information an advisor will need to properly examine where you are financially and to help you to prepare for where you will need to be in the days and years ahead. This can be a very beneficial exercise for both you and your spouse to complete as it will assist you in attaining a comprehensive financial awareness.

FINANCIAL AND ESTATE PLANNING INFORMATION FORM

(Please fill in approximate amounts prior to meeting with your advisor.
Also include your most recent tax return.)

CLIENT NAME _____

SOCIAL SECURITY # _____ CELL PHONE _____

E-MAIL ADDRESS _____ DATE OF BIRTH _____ Age _____

SPOUSE NAME _____

SOCIAL SECURITY # _____ CELL PHONE _____

E-MAIL ADDRESS: _____ DATE OF BIRTH _____ Age _____

MAILING ADDRESS _____

CITY _____ STATE _____ ZIP _____

HOME PHONE (_____)_____ BUSINESS PHONE (_____) _____

Do you have a current will?   Yes _____   No _____   Living Trust? Yes _____ No _____

Are you concerned about possible Nursing Home Expenses? Yes _____ No _____

AMOUNTS IN BANKS, SAVINGS & LOANS & CREDIT UNIONS (NON-IRA)
(i.e., Checking, Savings, Money Market)

	NAME OF INSTITUTION	TYPE OF ACCOUNT	MATURITY DATE	INTEREST RATE	APPROXIMATE BALANCE
1.					$
2.					$
3.					$
4.					$
5.					$
6.					$

IRA ACCOUNTS AND OTHER RETIREMENT ACCOUNTS

ACCOUNT TYPE & LOCATION (BANK, BROKER, EMPLOYER)	TYPE (401k, IRA, 403b, ETC.)	APPROXIMATE MARKET VALUE
1. _____	_____	$ _____
2. _____	_____	$ _____
3. _____	_____	$ _____
4. _____	_____	$ _____

Planned retirement date:_____ or if retired, date retired:_____

STOCKS AND BONDS (WHERE YOU HOLD CERTIFICATES YOURSELF)

NAME OF STOCK/BOND	NUMBER OF SHARES	APPROXIMATE MARKET VALUE
1. _____	_____	$ _____
2. _____	_____	$ _____
3. _____	_____	$ _____
4. _____	_____	$ _____

MUTUAL FUNDS AND/OR BROKERAGE ACCOUNTS
(Please bring in latest reports/statements)

NAME OF BROKERAGE FIRM OR MUTUAL FUND	NUMBER OF SHARES	APPROXIMATE MARKET VALUE
1. _____	_____	$ _____
2. _____	_____	$ _____
3. _____	_____	$ _____
4. _____	_____	$ _____
5. _____	_____	$ _____

PROMISSORY NOTES & TRUST DEEDS
(Where someone owes or is paying you on a note)

NAME OF DEBTOR	INTEREST RATE	APPROXIMATE BALANCE OF NOTE
1. _____	_____ %	$ _____
2. _____	_____ %	$ _____

RESIDENCE AND OTHER REAL ESTATE OWNED
(use another sheet if more space is needed)

PROPERTY ADDRESS	ORIGINAL COST	APPROX. VALUE	DEBT	NET CASH FLOW BEFORE DEPREC (if a rental)
1. _____	$ _____	$ _____	$ _____	$ _____
_____				
2. _____	$ _____	$ _____	$ _____	$ _____
_____				
3. _____	$ _____	$ _____	$ _____	$ _____
_____				

LIMITED OR GENERAL PARTNERSHIPS

NAME OF PARTNERSHIP	TYPE OF INVESTMENT	APPROXIMATE MARKET VALUE or AMOUNT INVESTED
1. _____	_____	$ _____
2. _____	_____	$ _____
3. _____	_____	$ _____

OTHER ASSETS

1. _____	$ _____
2. _____	$ _____
3. _____	$ _____

LIFE INSURANCE
(Please bring in policies and latest statements)

COMPANY	NAME OF INSURED	TYPE OF INSURANCE (WHOLE, LIFE, TERM)	APPROX. DEATH BENEFIT	LOAN AGAINST?
1. _____	_____	_____	$ _____	$ _____
2. _____	_____	_____	$ _____	$ _____
3. _____	_____	_____	$ _____	$ _____
4. _____	_____	_____	$ _____	$ _____

ANNUITIES
(Please bring in contracts and latest statements)

COMPANY	ANNUITANT/ OWNER	INTEREST RATE	APPROX. VALUE	DATE PURCHASED
1.		_____ %	$ _____	_____
2.		_____ %	$ _____	_____
3.		_____ %	$ _____	_____
4.		_____ %	$ _____	_____

HOUSEHOLD CASH FLOW

HUSBAND'S WAGES: $ _____ /YR   SOURCE: _____

WIFE'S WAGES: $ _____ /YR   SOURCE: _____

OTHER INCOME: 1. $ _____ /YR   SOURCE: _____

OTHER INCOME 2. $ _____ /YR   SOURCE: _____

WHAT ARE YOUR APPROXIMATE ANNUAL EXPENSES: $ _____

What are your primary financial concerns? List in order of importance.

_____

_____

How would you improve your financial situation if you could? Why?

_____

_____

_____

_____

_____

_____

_____

_____

_____

As a private pilot, checklists have helped me stay alive in the cockpit for over 25 years. I have found that **a short pencil is better than a long memory.**

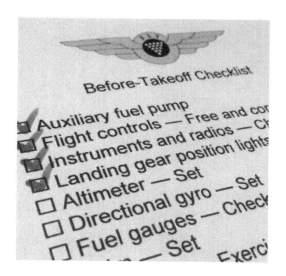

For that reason, I am a checklist fanatic. I insist that all the systems my administrative staff coordinate be monitored through checklists. Here is a quick checklist to help you further your attainment of a comprehensive financial awareness. This form will help you envision the estimated value of your estate. The following information is important; however, this exercise does not have to be completed to the precise penny. See if you can arrive at a rough ballpark estimate of your estate value.

VALUE OF ESTATE ASSETS

Market Value of Your Home .... $ _____

Market Value of Other Real Estate .... $ _____

Business Interest... $ _____

Oil, Gas, Mineral Interest.. $ _____

Automobiles.. $ _____

Boats .... $ _____

Motor Homes.. $ _____

Household Goods.. $ _____

Jewelry .... $ _____

Collections (Coin, Gun, Stamp, Antiquities, etc.) .... $ _____

Tools and Equipment .... $ _____

Life Insurance.. $ _____

Annuities... $ _____

Certificate of Deposit .... $ _____

Money Market Accounts .... $ _____

Government Bonds... $ _____

Stocks.. $ _____

Mutual Funds... $ _____

IRA/Roth/401k/403b/Pension/Deferred Compensation .... $ _____

Regular Savings .... $ _____

Checking Accounts .... $ _____

Expected Inheritance .... $ _____

APPROXIMATE VALUE OF YOUR ESTATE $ _____

Another element of the data-gathering process is to examine any liabilities or debts that are owed against any of your assets. To the side of each of the above assets, list any debt that you might owe and put brackets around the debt amount. This will be helpful in the financial plan section as you examine the definitions of estate terminology.

Your Personalized Financial Plan

Once the comprehensive data is gathered, the work begins for the advisor and the advisor's administrative assistant or planning team. Advisors throughout the investment advisory industry choose to structure their practices in a myriad of ways. There is no one right or wrong way when it comes to a chosen approach to staffing. Some advisors choose to work as solo practitioners in conjunction with your other advisors, such as your accountant and your estate planning attorney. Others choose to team up with other professionals within their own firms. The critical key is the advisor's knowledge and capacity to produce viable financial and investment advice.

A Comprehensive Financial Awareness will bring clarity to the following.

Gross Death Estate - the total of all assets, including life insurance death benefits, prior to the deduction of outstanding debts

Net Death Estate - the total of all assets, including life insurance death benefits, after the payment of all outstanding debts and final expenses

Gross Estate - the total of all assets minus life insurance death benefits

Net Worth - the total of all assets minus life insurance death benefits and all current liabilities

Not only will your personalized financial plan give you a comprehensive financial awareness, but also, it will provide guidance and future direction toward your financial goals. In the early days I would produce financial plans in fancy three ring binders that were 2- or 3-inches thick, filled with every imaginable frivolous graph and detail of a client's financial life. They were so thick and heavy that it became almost comical. We would laugh about doing financial planning "by the pound." I finally realized that no one, except for an occasional engineer, would ever read all that stuff. People took them home, stored them for a while and eventually threw them in the trash, hopefully after shredding them.

Once I realized the excessiveness of the binder, I began personalizing and summarizing in a simple two- to three-page letter, the power of these seven personal financial disciplines. To succeed, not only must I compile a financial plan, but also, I must make that plan understandable and transferable into viable action. For instance, having a comprehensive financial awareness of your current status still does not address "where you will need to be financially in days ahead." We will confront that question in the Retirement Planning chapter. One of my passions is to help someone know beyond a shadow of any doubt that his financial house is in order. Through implementing these seven principles, you can have that gratifying confidence and assurance.

Chapter Two

Discipline Two: Estate Planning

"I made my money the old fashioned way. I was very nice to a wealthy relative right before he died." --- Malcolm Forbes

Where There Is a Will, There May Still Be a Mess

A senior gentleman was asked, "How does your family like your new hearing aids?" He responded, "Oh, I haven't told them I got them yet. I just sit around and listen to their conversations, and so far, I have changed the beneficiary of my will three times."

The comprehensive financial awareness that you have attained through the data-gathering process answers the first question in estate planning: What do you have? Now we have to answer the second question: Where do you want it to go?

Estate Planning basically deals with those two questions: What do you have, and where do you eventually want it to go? Often the financial community has been guilty of pushing off your estate plan as some "final frontier." After they have gathered your assets under management and written all of the appropriate (or possibly inappropriate) insurance products, then they finally (and sometimes never) get around to addressing your estate planning needs. Well, personally, I believe that those needs must be addressed first thing after acquiring a comprehensive financial awareness. Why? Because it has everything in the world to do with how your assets are titled and registered. In my opinion, this is the foundation of the planning process. The greatest financial plans can unravel if the assets are not titled and registered properly. We will dig into this deeper later in this chapter. Eventually, in its completion, your financial plan should address all seven major financial disciplines: Comprehensive Financial Awareness, Estate Planning, Risk Management, Cash Management, Retirement Planning, Tax Strategies, and Asset Allocation. This is actually the sequence in which I prefer to address each of these issues. However, the sequence in which your advisor proceeds is not as critical as the fact that each discipline is properly completed.

Let's examine some of the components of a solid estate plan. As a Certified Estate Planner, I will address these issues from a "planning" perspective rather than from a legal or tax perspective. You should always consult with an attorney for any legal perspective and an accountant for tax issues. I have often heard people refer to probate and death taxes as if they are related. Actually probate has to do with determining the legal order of distribution of assets. Death taxes have to do with the Internal Revenue Service.

Are your assets properly titled? For many, that might involve trust planning in addition to a pour-over will, financial powers of attorney, health care powers of attorney, and an Advanced Directive which can include a living will and an appointment of health care proxy. Having a trust is not enough. You must have the assets deeded or titled into the trust registration name in order for it to accomplish its purpose.

Often, the initial attempt at estate planning is a basic "I love you" will. The intent could be, "If I die, everything goes to my spouse. If my spouse dies, everything goes to me, and when we both die, everything goes to our children." To put it simply, what most people are trying to do is pass all of their "stuff" (home, car, truck, boat, checking, savings, stocks, bonds, etc.) on to their heirs in an uncomplicated and inexpensive manner. With a will, when an individual dies, depending on the "registration" of the asset, the beneficiary should receive his rightful distribution, but only after probate. Probate might not be the most practical or cost-effective manner of getting the job done.

The probate process is basically a "proving process" to determine the eventual distribution of one's assets. In Latin, the word probate means "to prove." By consulting with your advisors, you can find alternatives to probate and possibly reduce some unnecessary litigation. Could a trust be a tool that is right for you? It is important for you to gain a basic understanding of these revocable and irrevocable estate planning tools. For simplicity's sake, we will say a "revocable" trust can be revoked, amended or changed, and an irrevocable trust cannot be as easily undone.

Living Probate

Some choose to hold assets in Joint Tenancy with Rights of Survivorship (JTWROS). A joint tenancy or joint tenancy with right of survivorship (JTWROS) is a type of registration in which co-owners have a *right of survivorship*, meaning that if one owner dies, that owner's interest in the property will pass to the surviving owner or owners and avoid probate, at least at the first owner's death. Another form of registration, Tenancy in Common (TIC), means that each owner, referred to as a tenant in common, is regarded as owning separate and distinct shares of the same property. When assets are held in Tenancy in Common (TIC), co-owners own equal shares but their interests may differ in size. This form of ownership is most common where the co-owners are not married or have contributed different amounts to the purchase of the property. Tenants in Common have no right of survivorship; therefore, succession issues become more complex.

Married couples often register their assets in Joint Tenants with Rights of Survivorship (JTWROS) without considering the potential concerns of one or both of them becoming incapacitated, incoherent or incognizant. The healthy spouse, if faced with the need to liquidate certain assets in order to pay potential medical expenses, may possibly face conservatorship or guardianship issues commonly referred to as "living probate." Living probate cases have surged in recent years due to the demographic age wave of the baby-boomers caring for the builder generations Alzheimer's, dementia, and senile concerns.

Every form of registration has its advantages and disadvantages. It is important for you and your successor to understand the differences between forms. There are issues that a joint tenant could face in managing assets when his spouse becomes incapacitated or incoherent. *There can also be complications that arise when a spouse dies and adult children are chosen as joint tenants to the assets.*

- Have you created a gift that exceeds the current gift tax exemption amount?

- Now, if you gift the asset back to the original owner, have you created a second   gift?

- What if your adult child has credit complications (like "MasterCard Mania") and you add her as a joint tenant to your assets? Could their creditors attach your assets?

- If your child is innocently involved in an auto accident, which results in a fatality in the other vehicle, have we not potentially encumbered our own assets by having them listed as a joint tenant?

- Do you have your estate plan structured in such a manner as to take full advantage of the existing estate tax rules? Could a married couple not lose one of the death tax exemptions if they do not plan in advance of the death of the first spouse?

- If you gift an appreciated asset, such as real estate or stock, to your children in advance of your death, will they not miss out on the step-up in tax basis that they might receive if you had waited and let them inherit it upon your demise?

Here is quick example on the appreciated asset dilemma. John Senior purchased a piece of real estate years ago for $30,000. Today it is worth $100,000, and he decides to gift the deed to his adult son, Junior. John Senior does not realize that Junior now assumes the original cost basis in the property. Shortly after the deed transfer, John Senior dies. Junior then sells the property and realizes a $70,000 capital gain, thus resulting in capital gains taxes. Based on current tax code, if John Senior had waited to pass the property on to Junior at his death, for instance through his trust, then Junior would have received a "step-up" in the cost basis to current market value. Junior could have then sold the property without a realized capital gain and saved himself thousands – if only they had known. This simple mistake occurs constantly due to so many refusing to seek proper counsel.

We also have to consider how our procrastination to act may cause us to forfeit certain grandfathered privileges in this ever-changing political environment. How do we plan with the uncertainty of future decisions that Congress will make? I strongly recommend your thorough consideration of each of these issues before making hasty uninformed decisions.

Death Probate

We have addressed some of the "Living Probate" issues. Now let's look at the death side of probate. If an individual dies holding "probatable" assets in his name, then basically the only way to transition those assets to the rightful heirs is through a process we will call "Death Probate." There are several issues to consider.

- In some states the legal community can charge both statutory fees and reasonable charges. Other states will only allow reasonable charges.

- Delays can take up to a year. I heard one individual say that his uncle's probate took six years.

- Emotional stress is already heightened due to the loss of a loved one. Court proceedings can be even more exhausting.

- Public notifications must be filed regarding the receipt of claims and the payment of claims against the estate.

- Contest can arise from disgruntled heirs.

- Out-of-state assets may be faced with probate in the state where the assets are held in addition to dealing with the home state.

- Control is impossible since the decedent is not available to handle matters in the manner he might have chosen.

When you choose to create a revocable living trust, all of your probatable "stuff" (home, car, truck, boat, checking, savings, stocks, bonds, etc.) can be titled into the trust. Re-registering or re-titling the assets into the trust is often referred to as "funding the trust." This step is critically important to the validity of your estate plan. An unfunded trust is as useless as the paper upon which it is written. At times people think that since their documents were drafted, their plan is in place. That's not true. An unfunded trust is an empty shell. Getting your assets properly titled into your trust is what makes it all work. If all of your probatable assets are properly titled in your trust, then your trust becomes your new form of ownership. I like to think of it in this way: if I do not own anything, then there is nothing to probate. If your trust owns your assets upon the death of both trustors, typically husband and wife, then the assets will be distributed directly to your heirs, bypassing the probate process.

Some assets will bypass probate by contract. Your retirement plans, IRAs, 401(k), 403(b), Roth IRA, Simple IRA, SEP, life insurance, annuities, bank POD (payable on death) or TOD (transfer on death) all have beneficiary designations. Beneficiary designations are direct contracts with the issuing firm. Beneficiary designations supersede your will or trust instructions. We will discuss this further later in this chapter.

At the time of this writing, there are no federal estate taxes due at the first death of a spouse. There is an unlimited marital deduction for federal estate taxes. However, it is shortly after the second death that the IRS will put its hand out, requesting payment of taxes on assets in excess of the then current exemption amount. Suppose with me for a moment that you have predeceased your spouse. She remains behind, healthy and happy. Due to your willingness to plan in advance, the trust was prepared in a manner that now affords her the privilege of capturing two federal estate tax exemption amounts. Therefore, whatever the current federal estate tax exemption amount happens to be, she can place that amount into your trust, the decedent's trust, and the remainder of the estate can be held in her trust, the survivor's trust, free from federal estate taxes. There are other advanced planning tools that your advisers can prepare for larger estates that will not be discussed here due to time and the ongoing evolution of such and the ever-changing tax environment.

Imagine your surviving spouse, in a nice new vehicle, rolling on through the years, pulling two open trailers, each containing the full federal estate tax exemption amount. What if someone comes along and falls in love with your spouse's trailers? *I would hope and expect that if I died today, my spouse would remarry. However, I would not want her new husband's children to inherit all of the assets and leave our children out in the cold.* Proper planning allows you to secure your line of succession. The decedent's trust becomes irrevocable upon the first spouse's death. This brings an assurance that no one can undo what you've done. Your surviving spouse can invade the decedent's trust for her own health, education, maintenance and support. However, no one else can do so.

Six Easy Steps to a Complete Estate Plan

Step One: Determine the Goal

Begin with the end in mind. Do you want to retain the power to revoke, amend or change this plan? What is it that you are ultimately attempting to accomplish? Are you simply wanting to transition smoothly and in a cost-effective manner, the eventual control of the assets of your estate to a surviving spouse and finally to your heirs? Are you planning in advance in order to avoid the unnecessary process of living probate or death probate? Are you comfortable with eventual lump sum distributions at the time of your and your spouse's deaths, or do you want some sequential spendthrift provision to pay out over time to your heirs? Congratulations on pursuing your goals. They can all be attained through a properly-constructed estate plan.

Step Two: Gather the Data

Make a list of the overall estate assets. See Chapter One, Comprehensive Financial Awareness, in order to learn more on gathering the needed data. You will need to determine what you have and how and where the assets are currently registered. Ultimately, certain assets will become registered in the estate plan name. In addition to assets, the data-gathering process will include certain family biographical information and the current and eventual players (parties) of the plan.

Step Three: Determine the Players (Parties)

In the typical "I love you" basic estate plan, where everything goes to a surviving spouse and eventually to the heirs, if you choose to utilize a revocable living trust, then the players may take on the following titles and roles:

Title	Role	Players/Parties
Trustors	Create the Trust	Husband/Wife
Trustees	Manage the Trust	Husband/Wife
Initial Beneficiaries	Receive all Benefits	Husband/Wife
------------After the Death of Both Trustors------------		
Successor Trustees Trustee	Distribute the Trust	Heirs/or Corporate
Remaining Beneficiaries	Receive Remain. Benefits	Heirs/Charities

Obviously, it is important to have a basic understanding of the title and role of the various players or parties of a trust estate plan. Terminology in estate planning can be confusing because there are certain terms that are often used interchangeably. For instance, trustor, creator, grantor or settlor all typically referred to the party that creates the trust. Trustees manage the trust. Beneficiaries receive the benefit of the trust.

Step Four: Draft the Documents and Execute the Plan

I strongly advocate hiring an estate planning attorney to draft your estate plan documents. In addition to drafting your trust, which becomes your new form of holding title to certain assets, the attorney will also prepare additional essential documents to complete your plan.

The Trust - The trust holds the registration of certain assets to avoid both future probate concerns and conservator and guardianship concerns, minimize the potential federal estate tax issues, and help secure a proper line of succession after the death of one or both trustors.

Power of Attorney for Finances - The POA for finances determines who will make financial decisions on your behalf, if needed, regarding assets held outside the trust. People are often confused, thinking that all assets will be re-titled to the trust. That is incorrect. Certain assets, such as an IRA or retirement account, will continue in your individual account registration while you are living. To actually re-title them into a trust name would create an immediate, possibly severe, unwanted tax consequence. For IRAs and retirement plans, the spouse will usually continue as the primary beneficiary with either the children or the trust as the contingent beneficiary. The same could hold true for other beneficiary designations such as life insurance and annuities. However, it is best to consult your estate planner in this regard as well. If an uninformed financial advisor tells you to put the word "estate" as your beneficiary designation, they unknowingly could throw a non-probatable asset back into probate court. Also, as we stated earlier, assets with transfer on death (TOD) or payable on death (POD) designations will bypass probate and go directly to the living beneficiary designee.

Power of Attorney for Healthcare - The POA for healthcare determines who will make your healthcare decisions in the event that you become incoherent, incognizant or incapacitated to the extent that you are unable to make such decisions. Again, your spouse often serves first in this role, followed by children. I often smile and encourage people to consider a compassionate person for this role.

Pour-Over Will - You may think I'm beating up on wills because they go through probate; however, I am actually saying that you need one. In the event that you inadvertently leave an asset out of your trust, which should have been titled into it, the pour-over will pours the asset into the trust rather than allowing a probate court to choose where it goes. That does not mean it will avoid probate. It just means that, ultimately, the trust still determines the eventual distribution of the asset.

Advance Directive and Health Care Proxy - You should also consider including your state specific **Advance Directive** along with your other estate planning documents. Since the document does vary from state to state, I will avoid specifics here. However, this medical advance directive could include both a **Living Will**, often inaccurately confused with a living trust and an **Appointment of Health Care Proxy**. In simplistic terms a living will can give you the opportunity to state to your physicians your personal intentions if you are ever faced with terminal illness, persistent unconsciousness or end stage condition. The document deals with your desire regarding the issue of food and hydration and life-sustaining treatment. Your Appointment of Health Care Proxy can designate the individual who will make these tough end-of-life decisions on your behalf if you have not authorized your own Advance Directive. Please consider taking those tough decisions off the shoulders of your loved ones by acknowledging and authorizing your personal desires and properly planning in advance.

Step Five: Re-titling the Assets (Funding the Trust)

The primary purpose of your trust is to avoid probate of your estate. In order to accomplish this, you must transfer the ownership of your assets into the trust. In addition, all assets you acquire from here on, which could face probate, must be titled in the name of your trust.

Control over Your Assets in a Revocable Trust

As long as you are not incompetent or incapacitated, you retain control over all of the revocable trust assets. In a revocable trust, you can be the Trustee. In the event you become incompetent or incapacitated, the Successor Trustee will manage the assets for you. When you take title to an asset (anything with a title or an account number), you should title that asset in your trust name as in the following example:

John E. Doe and Jane C. Doe, Trustees of the John E. and Jane C. Doe Revocable Trust dtd

_____.

HOW TO TRANSFER TITLES INTO YOUR TRUST

1.   UNTITLED TANGIBLE PERSONAL PROPERTY

Untitled tangible personal property includes furniture, household goods, furnishings, silverware, antiques, china, jewelry, etc. These items do not have any type of title or registration. The transfer of these assets to your trust is accomplished through an **Assignment of Tangible Property,** which your plan should include as one of its documents.

Untitled tangible personal property used for a trade or business such as machinery, livestock, farm equipment, tools, etc. should also be transferred to your trust through an Assignment of Tangible Property.

2.   TITLED TANGIBLE PERSONAL PROPERTY

Titled tangible personal property includes cars, motorcycles, motor homes, airplanes, boats and boat trailers. These assets have titles or certificates of ownership. Certain states probate these assets. Ask your estate planner if this applies to your resident state. In order to place these assets into your trust, you should have the titles reissued in the name of your trust. In order to have titles reissued in the name of the trust, your estate planner will need the original title, a copy of your insurance verification and a copy of your driver's license.

3.   REAL PROPERTY AND MINERAL DEEDS

Real property includes all real estate. To transfer the ownership, you will need the original warranty deed or quit claim deed. Your estate planning attorney will then prepare new deeds, which will be authorized and notarized at the time of your trust execution. Do not forget to address any mineral deeds as well. You never know when Jed Clampett might be shooting at some food and up from the ground comes a bubbling crude. (If you do not know the meaning of my previous statement, you are probably too young to be reading this book.)

4.   STOCKS AND BONDS

You will need to provide the estate planner with all stocks and bonds to transfer the stock into the trust name.

5.   UNREGISTERED BONDS

Unregistered municipal bonds and unregistered treasury bonds may be assigned to your trust through an Assignment (much like the Assignments used to transfer tangible personal property).

6.   SOLE PROPRIETORSHIPS AND LIMITED OR GENERAL PARTNERSHIPS

Assignments are also used to transfer the ownership of business assets such as sole proprietorships and limited or general partnerships.

7.   BANK ACCOUNTS

The ownership of your bank accounts should be transferred to your trust. The bank will ask you to execute a new signature card. The account ownership again should read as this example:

John E. Doe or Jane C. Doe, Trustees of the John E. and Jane C. Doe Revocable Trust, dated _____.

Ownership is determined by what appears on the bank records and signature card – not what is written on your check. Your checks can be changed to read the trust name, or you can leave them in your individual name, whichever appeals to you. In addition, the bank should allow you to sign your checks without the word "trustee" after your signature. The bank will probably request a copy of your **Memorandum of Trust Agreement.** The Memorandum of Trust is basically a brief synopsis or skeletal summary of the pertinent data of your trust that a financial institution might need for verification purposes.

8.   CERTIFICATES OF DEPOSIT

Certificates of Deposit can be transferred into your trust simply by supplying the bank with a written request (i.e., a letter). The bank may request a copy of your Memorandum of Trust Agreement.

9.   SAFE DEPOSIT BOXES

The ownership of your safe deposit box can be transferred to your trust by supplying the bank with a written request (i.e., a letter).

10.   GOVERNMENT BONDS

U.S. government bonds such as Series E Bonds can be transferred to your trust by taking your original bonds to a national banking institution that issues bonds. The bank officer should be able to assist you in transferring your bonds to your trust. The bonds should be titled as the following example:

John E. Doe and Jane C. Doe, Trustees of the John E. and Jane C. Doe Revocable Trust, dated

_____.

12. PROMISSORY NOTES AND MORTGAGES

Promissory Notes and security instruments such as mortgages on real estate should be assigned to your trust using an Assignment. The assignment could read as follows:

We hereby sell, assign and convey to John E. Doe and Jane C. Doe, Trustees of the John E. and Jane C. Doe Revocable Trust, dated_____, or their successors in trust, all of our right, title and interest in and to the following:

(Put description of note or mortgage here.) Remember that these are promissory notes that individuals owe you, not notes that you owe someone else.

13. LIFE INSURANCE

On your life insurance policies, you may retain your spouse as your primary beneficiary, and your trust can be the contingent beneficiary. This serves in the event that you are both involved in a common disaster. Your insurance agent should be able to help you obtain a change of beneficiary form if one cannot be located on the company's website.

If your estate is approaching the current federal estate tax exemption amount, you should strongly consider setting up an **ILIT (Irrevocable Life Insurance Trust).** The irrevocable trust could then hold the ownership of your life insurance policies, thus removing the death benefit value from your estate and reducing the size of your gross death estate. This reduction in the size of your estate can lower the estate taxes.

14. IRAS AND RETIREMENT PLANS

Proceeds from IRAs and qualified retirement plans pass to a named beneficiary. It is very important that you remain owner, your spouse remains primary beneficiary and only the contingent beneficiary designation may change. Changing the ownership of an IRA or qualified retirement plan will trigger a taxable event. If you are wanting to include a charity in the eventual distribution of your retirement plan, consult with your advisers first.

Step Six: Maintaining the Plan

Trust Maintenance - My wife laughed when I hit midlife and went out and bought a Harley-Davidson motorcycle. She wasn't laughing because of the way I looked in head-to-toe leather. In fact, we bought her leathers as well (and man was she hot). She laughed because I, the Certified Estate Planner, got so excited about the motorcycle that I forgot to tell the dealership to title it into the name of my trust. Since I live in a state that even probates motorcycles, I had to later make a trip by the tag agency in order to get it titled into trust.

Trust maintenance is as simple as keeping it funded. Please remember that the ownership of your assets must be changed to reflect your trust as the new owner. Any asset that does not pass to a named beneficiary by operation of law or any asset that has not been titled in your trust name with you as trustee of your trust will go through probate.

Income Taxes - For federal and most state income tax purposes, it is not necessary to file a separate tax return for your revocable trust as long as you serve as your own trustee. Where the person who created the trust has reserved the right to terminate the trust, as you have, the income passes through the trust and is reported directly on the grantor's 1040. Revocable trusts use the social security number of the grantor instead of a new taxpayer identification number issued by the IRS.

Disability or Illness - If you are faced with disability or illness, you may want to consider discussing other estate planning techniques with your advisors to protect your estate from unnecessary losses.

Death - In the event of a death, you (as a surviving spouse) or your Successor Trustee should contact a qualified professional who can instruct you on what steps to take to ensure the smooth transition of closing out the estate. You may want to review this section from time to time. It contains many answers to some of the common questions regarding revocable trusts.

What Your Executor/Successor Trustee Needs to Know

I was never brazen enough to buy the plaque and hang it in our office, but there sure were times I thought about it. The plaque said, LACK OF PLANNING ON YOUR PART DOES NOT CONSTITUTE AN EMERGENCY ON MY PART! There have been several occasions when I have had to scurry to the hospital, even the intensive care unit, to assist in the execution of documents that should have been finalized years earlier. I am grateful to have grown up in a loving pastor's home, which prepared me for facing life's complications with compassion.

Needless to say there are many more issues that need to be covered surrounding all the estate planning scenarios. A loving gesture would be to plan in advance in order to simplify the inevitable process that our executor/successor/trustee must face.

1. The duties of an executor can seem overwhelming. Here are some of the possible responsibilities:
2. Find the last will and read it.
3. File a petition with the court to probate the will.
4. Assemble all of the decedent's assets.
5. Take possession of the safe deposit box contents.
6. Consult with the banks and savings and loans in the area to find all accounts of the deceased. Also check

7. for cash and other valuables hidden around the home.
8. Transfer all securities to his or her name (as executor) and continue to collect dividends and interest on behalf of the heirs of the deceased.
9. Find, inventory and protect household and personal effects and other personal property.
10. Collect all life insurance proceeds payable to the estate.
11. Find and inventory all real estate deeds, mortgages, leases   and tax information. Provide immediate management for rental properties.
12. Arrange ancillary administration for out-of-state
13. property.
14. Collect monies owed to the deceased and check
15. interests in estates of other deceased persons.
16. Find and safeguard business interests, valuables,
17. personal property, important papers, the residence, etc.
18. Inventory all assets and arrange for appraisal of those for which it is appropriate.
19. Determine liquidity needs. Assemble bookkeeping records. Review investment portfolio. Sell appropriate assets.
20. Pay valid claims against the estate. Reject improper claims and defend the estate if necessary.
21. Pay state and federal taxes due.
22. File income tax returns for the decedent and the
    a. estate.

23. Determine whether the estate qualifies for special use valuation under IRC Sec. 2032A, the qualified family-owned business interest deduction under IRC Sec. 2057 of deferral of estate taxes under IRC Secs. 6161 or 6166.
24. If the surviving spouse is not a U.S. citizen, consider a qualified domestic trust to defer the payment of federal estate taxes.
25. File federal estate tax return and state death and/or inheritance tax return.

Here is a sobering thought. Someday, someone else will give away all of your assets. While you have the opportunity, consider taking the necessary steps to ensure your assets are distributed in the manner you would choose.

Chapter Three

Discipline Three: Risk Management

"Risk management is the protective component of a sound financial plan." ---John Gillespie

It is difficult to imagine working a lifetime, accumulating money and property, and waking up one morning to discover that all is lost. You may wonder if that is really possible. Not only is it possible, but, it actually happens to good hard-working people. Without proper protection mechanisms in place, you, too, could become a victim of a catastrophic occurrence.

The Protective Component

Risk management is the protective component of a sound financial plan. It addresses protection from the risk of potential financial devastation, and focuses on the primary concerns of estate preservation and income replacement. There are more risk management concerns than we will have time to address in this book. For the sake of time, I will focus my writings in a couple of areas. However, let me list some of the risk management concerns that you may need to address.

1) Exposing Your Assets to Someone Else's Creditors (ex: Joint Tenants - we addressed this in Chapter 2: Estate Planning): Never take on risks that do not and should not belong to you. Why own a vehicle that someone else is driving? If that person is 18 years old or possibly 98 years old, do you really want your name on the title of the vehicle they are driving? Consider either selling or giving the vehicle to them.

2) Cosigning for Liabilities: Be extremely cautious to avoid placing yourself in unnecessary, potentially harmful contractual obligations.

3) Inadequate Corporate Legal Structure: Inasmuch as possible, attempt to separate your corporate and professional life from your personal affairs. If you are an officer, you are probably liable.

4) Umbrella Coverage: Pure liability coverage shields assets more broadly and *in addition to* primary coverage. See your Property and Casualty agent.

5) Professional Liability Insurance (PLI): Also called Errors and Omissions Insurance (E&O), PLI helps to protect professional advice- and service-providing individuals and companies from bearing the full cost of defending claims of negligence, potentially resulting in civil lawsuit.

6) Health Insurance: Potential catastrophic healthcare occurrences can lead to medical bankruptcy. Consistent, routine, proactive, preventative healthcare can help to protect you from avoidable healthcare concerns.

7) Disability Insurance (DI): DI is also known as Disability Income Insurance. If injury, illness or psychological disorders cause impairment or incapacity to work, DI can address the financial shortfall.

8) Property and Casualty Insurance (P&C): Insurance companies can apply the law of large numbers to cover potential property and accidental losses to help indemnify (make whole again) their insured policyholders.

9) Life Insurance: Life insurance was originally called death insurance, and companies had a difficult time selling it. Its name was changed to life insurance, and it thereby became one of the wealthiest industries in the world. The primary purposes of life insurance, in the event of a death, should be to replace the loss of income, repay outstanding loan obligations and eventually address estate distribution concerns.

10) Long-Term Care Insurance (LTC): LTC addresses the expenses arising from the incapacity to complete the six activities of daily living (ADL's): feeding, bathing, toileting, continence, transferring and dressing.

My First Risk Management Encounter

My first exposure to risk management concerns was in Nashville, Tennessee at Trevecca Nazarene University, my alma mater. I was there from 1973 to 1977. My wife and I married in 1975, and an insurance agent came over to talk to us about saving for retirement. He explained to me the "virtues" (his word) of owning an insurance plan that contained a savings component. The bottom line was that he was trying to sell me a $10,000 whole life insurance policy. Wow, I was so impressed that I asked him to make it $30,000 instead. He delightedly completed the application and in a few weeks delivered the policy. After a couple of years, a friend sat me down and explained that the particular policy I bought was actually extremely expensive and highly inadequate. He explained the difference in the $30,000 whole life policy I had purchased and how I could own $150,000 of term insurance for the same premium. The savings component of this specific whole life policy was a pathetic attempt at building any significant savings for my future. So, needless to say, I gladly replaced the whole life insurance with term. Now, in the event of my death, I had immediately increased the death benefit of my policy. My wife would receive five times more, without paying additional premium, with just the stroke of a signature on a different application. The thought occurred to me, "Maybe I should begin sleeping with one eye open." Not really. With the college debt owed in the 1970s, I was excited to know it would be covered and that there would still be funds left for my wife.

The term insurance agent then went on to introduce me to the investment industry. My wife and I had begun monthly systematic investments that eventually paid off our debt, gave us funds for a house down payment, educated our children at notable universities and built our retirement portfolio. I will deal with the investment process in later chapters.

Fast forward the clock to 1982. I arrived in Oklahoma City, Oklahoma on a corporate transfer. Within a few months of my arrival, a friend introduced me to a financial services advisor who confirmed that my financial plan was on a sound foundation. What he said, however, that intrigued me was that the majority of people were headed in the wrong direction and paying excessive amounts for outdated strategies. I have always been open-minded to opportunity and willing to question tradition. I accepted the challenge that year to give up a comfortable corporate career with a well-established, publicly-traded company and begin the transition, initially part-time, into the financial services industry. Knowing that there were insurance and securities examinations to pass and licenses to attain, I began methodically working toward a newly established goal.

The words of a wise, more mature mentor within the corporation that I would eventually leave actually helped to set my career transition into motion. I will never forget the conversation we had and the words he shared. He said, "Young man, it is not important that anyone know where you are going except for you and your spouse." He went on to say, "Make a plan and work your plan." Through the years I have watched many attempt to start businesses that did not understand that principle. They just jumped out of one career to another ill-equipped and unprepared. I do not believe you "go" into business. I believe you "grow" into business. The chances of success are greatly enhanced if you have grown to your inevitable place of transition. Having a vision of what can be is the key component to a successful future. What started in 1982, as acquiring a state insurance license, eventually resulted in additional Investment Securities Registrations of Series 6, 7, 24, 26, 63 and 65, CEP, and RFC designations. Today, along with a strong administrative team, a brilliant chief investment officer and cofounder of a proprietary tactical active allocation process, Registered Investment Advisors now hire us to manage their clients' portfolios.

Vision enables a person with the power to give up who he is in order to become all he can be. Hopefully, you will acquire a working knowledge of The Power of Seven Personal Financial Disciplines. Through your personal vision and with the help of your advisors, you will be able to skillfully implement these financial success strategies.

A Financial and Spiritual Conversion

In March 1984, I sat down with a friend to discuss a financial plan. For confidentiality purposes, we will change his name to Terry. Terry's story was very similar to mine except that the numbers were different. He had purchased a $150,000 whole life insurance policy. Applying the concept of "buy term and invest the difference," I was able to increase the death benefit of his coverage to $300,000 term life for less premium than he was paying for the whole life. I insisted clients never cancel a policy until they knew the new one was issued. Terry's application was approved, and I delivered the policy. That week the two of us attended a CBMC, Christian Businessmen's Connection, prayer breakfast. Through the presentation of another friend and Christian businessman, Dr. Herman Reese, DDS, Terry made a powerful spiritual decision to accept Jesus Christ as his Lord and Savior. He found a new sense of peace in his life. I was delighted that we now shared the same faith. When we walked out of the CBMC event, Terry mentioned that he would come by my office that afternoon to finalize the investment portion of his plan. The appointment time came and went. Terry never showed. I assumed he had either forgotten the appointment or was consumed in a more urgent issue. The following day I decided to call his home to see if we could reschedule our meeting. When his wife answered she distraughtly said, "Oh, John, you must not have heard." "Terry was hit head-on yesterday by a drunk driver on North May Avenue." It seemed as though the earth stopped moving for a moment as I struggled to compose my emotions. The next few days seemed like a blur. In less than two weeks, Terry passed away. I found myself sitting in the pallbearers' vehicle on our way to the cemetery holding back my own tears. Terry and his lovely wife had a handsome son, age 7. Naturally, Terry's financial story, which was truly amazing, remained confidentially silent. His spiritual story, which was truly miraculous, was the talk of the funeral. My friend Herman Reese spoke and masterfully delivered the eulogy.

Sometimes in life we are given another chance to get things right. Assurance of where you are going spiritually is the single most important thing you can have. It always trumps financial preparedness. However, financial preparedness is a form of wrapping your arms of love around your surviving spouse and children when you are no longer there to do so.

Do You Really Need It?

Whether or not you need life insurance coverage could be dependent on the answer to a few questions:

1) Do you have any outstanding debts?

2) Would anyone be dependent on your income if you died today?

3) Would your premature death create a hardship on anyone left behind?

4) Would your death create potential estate tax concerns at any point in the future?

5) Do you have need to carve out a specific financial distribution to a certain beneficiary in the future?

6) Are you attempting to leverage an eventual gift to charity?

If you answered "no" to all of the above questions and your total gross death estate is of sufficient size that you have become self-insured, then you might not need life insurance. However, if you answered yes to any of the above questions, be sure to seek proper counsel.

What Is the Right Amount of Coverage?

There is no set magic formula for determining the proper amount of coverage you should own. The most likely answer is found when you follow the preceding questions with another question: how much? For instance, it's easy to know how much it would take to pay off your debt. As to replacing your income, some industry analysts say you should have five times your annual income in death benefit. Some analysts say 10 times your annual income. The real answer lies in how many years you would want to replace your income to your remaining beneficiary.

Types of Life Insurance Coverage

This is by no means a definitive explanation of each form of life insurance protection. These will be generic definitions for you to use as a reference point when you consult with your advisors.

Annual Renewable Term (ART) - level death benefit, no savings component, low-cost initial entry, premiums increase annually, also referred to as **Yearly Renewable Term (YRT)**

5/10/15/20/25/30 Year Level Term - level death benefit, no savings component, level premium for the designated period, premiums increase at the end of each designated period

Decreasing Term - decreasing death benefit, often paired with a debt pay-off period such as a mortgage, sometimes called mortgage cancellation insurance, no savings component, level premium

Permanent Life - coverage remains in place until policy matures or owner fails to pay premiums, contains a cash value component, typically either whole life, fixed indexed life, universal life, limited pay or endowment

Whole Life - level death benefit, cash value component, premiums level for life in most cases, higher premiums than term at younger ages, some view whole life death benefits as simply paying back to the insured's beneficiary a decreasing term payout plus the accumulated cash value of the policy that equals the level death benefit, typically have surrender charges in earlier years of the policy

Universal Life - combines permanent coverage with flexible premium along with either traditional fixed universal (which has interest sensitive cash values tied to the general fund of the insurance company) or equity indexed universal (which ties the cash value returns to a myriad of stock or bond market indices) or variable universal (which ties the cash value returns to investment securities subaccounts, level death benefits (typically option A) or increasing death benefits (typically option B), depending on which option was chosen); will remain in effect as long as the premiums are sufficient to cover the mortality expenses, administrative expenses and optional rider expenses; typically have surrender charges in earlier years of the policy

Limited Pay - permanent coverage, level death benefit, cash value component, policy becomes paid up at some predetermined future date with no additional premiums necessary, some plans pay up in 10 years, 20 years or at age 65

Endowment Life - permanent coverage, level death benefit, cash value component where the cash value equals the death benefit face amount at a certain age; premiums are higher than whole life or universal life due to the shortened payment period; tax laws over the years have squeezed the tax shelter component requiring a certain death benefit to cash value ratio; if excessive premiums caused the plan to violate a calculated threshold, the policy becomes a modified endowment and would then be treated like an annuity or IRA.

Survivorship Life - permanent coverage on a husband and wife, with the death benefit not paying until the second death, also called **Second-To-Die Insurance**; with the unlimited marital exclusion, estate taxes are not due until after the death of the second parent; families often use Survivorship Life death benefits to eventually pay the estate taxes at the time of the surviving parents death; premiums are typically less for a Second-to-Die policy rather than buying separate policies on each parent

How to Protect Your Investment Portfolio from a Cruel, Debilitating Disease

In 2003, my father-in-law, a kind, gentle, unassuming man, after struggling with pulmonary fibrosis, slipped from this earth to his heavenly home. My mother-in-law, a strong, witty, vivacious lady, continued on in good health. During that year she turned 80 years of age. She began leaning on her adult children, my wife and her two siblings, to help with her financial decisions. After discussing her potential long-term care concerns with my wife, I made a phone call to each of my wife's siblings. The phone call went like this. "I'm just the son-in-law here, but we might want to consider the fact that this is the last year (age 80) that Mom can purchase long-term care insurance. Give it some thought while she is still in good health." The family agreed to examine some quotes and apply for coverage. The long-term care policy was issued, and Mom continued on in good health for six years. Then, after its diagnosis, Alzheimer's began to take its toll. *You never think someone so physically healthy will become so helpless.* Once two of the six activities of daily living (ADL's: feeding, bathing, toileting, transferring, continence and dressing) were no longer functioning, the long-term care benefit payout began. In many plans like hers, cognitive impairment supersedes the required ADLs and triggers the benefit payout. At the time of this writing, the family struggles daily with the final stages of Alzheimer's. The services of hospice have been activated. None of us know what tomorrow holds in regard to our future health. Statistics have accelerated regarding end-of-life concerns to the point that we are now told that one out of two people will someday need long-term care assistance. If your family investment portfolio is not of sufficient size to handle the potential multi-year required expenses of an end-of-life catastrophic health occurrence, for you and your spouse, consider long-term care insurance.

Chapter Four

Discipline Four: Cash Management

"Too many people spend money they haven't earned...to buy things they don't want...to impress people they don't like."
---Will Rogers

You Can Spend It All

Through the years I have consulted families from every socioeconomic level. I have witnessed the most ridiculous, unthinkable cases of financial management. You have probably heard people say, "Oh, they have so much money they could never spend it all." Well, I can promise you that there is no such human being alive. You can spend it all. The exhaustion of capital (interpreted as spending every dime you have) is no respecter of your starting point or accumulated amount. The problem is much bigger, deeper, higher and wider than any amount of money. The problem is threefold.

The Three Greatest Financial Problems in the World

The three greatest financial problems in the world today are financial ignorance, wrong attitudes and poor planning. Let's examine each one of these.

1) Financial Ignorance is not the same as stupidity. It is simply a lack of knowledge. Many people have chosen to neglect receiving the necessary financial education that is reasonably required to function with financial stability. That is why receiving an overnight fortune through an inheritance, lawsuit settlement or winning the lottery is truly not the answer. One statistic stated that "90% of lotto winners after 12 months have no family, no friends, and no money left." It does not have to be that way. Stupidity is not the problem. Ignorance is the problem.

2) Wrong Attitudes are often evidenced in uncontrollable spending and the abuse of credit. You must get out of debt and stay out of debt. The abuse of credit often begins quite innocently, yet it very rapidly it grows and very tragically it ends. It often ends in either bankruptcy court or divorce court. The problem with credit cards is not only the outrageous interest rates that enslave the borrower to the lender but also the fact that even if you pay them off in 27 days to avoid the interest, you still have a tendency to overspend. When you swipe a piece of plastic through the machine, you do not feel the same degree of damage as you do when you take out your wallet and shell out cold hard cash. (I am not sure why people call it cold hard cash. It's really warm, fluffy and green.) I have never met a couple who fell madly in love, got married, and said, "Let's see what kind of miserable financial mess we can make of our lives." No. They always wake up and ask, "How in the world did this happen?" The answer is simple. They were spending money they hadn't earned. There is a solution to the problem of uncontrollable spending and the abuse of credit. It is the B word. No matter who you are and no matter how much you make, anyone who is financially stable lives on a *budget*. For instance, if you do not understand that you have a car payment for the rest of your life (even if you do not owe a balance on a car), then you do not understand the power of having a budget. Let's suppose you are paying $600 per month on a car payment. When the car is paid off, you have to continue putting that same money into your auto allowance category each month or you will never feel the joy of paying cash for one. My wife and I implemented this practice early in our marriage. I don't mind telling you it took years to get in the position to enjoy the fruit from planting that seed. Then the day arrived. I walked into the dealership and negotiated harder and more effectively than I ever had. I could hardly wait for the salesman to ask me how I planned to pay for it. I had been practicing the answer. He asked "Mr. Gillespie, how would you like to pay for this?" I proudly responded, "Like a hamburger." That next month, money still went into the auto allowance category. Years later, still goes there and will this month also. I apply the same principle toward the airplane as well.

**3)	Poor Planning** is the third problem. You have probably heard it said that most people don't plan to fail; they just fail to plan. I mentioned in chapter 3 how important it is to "make a plan and work your plan." I strongly believe that if you don't know where you are going, you will probably wind up somewhere else. This entire book is dedicated to planning; therefore, I will move on without belaboring its importance. However, I will say this as to how critical your plan is to your future financial destination: It serves like the flange on the wheel of a train. It keeps you on track when you go around life's financial curves.

Record Keeping

Your CPA or accountant would love the fact that you are reading this right now. Recordkeeping enables financial awareness. It allows your advisors to protect you from undocumented, invalidated data. Recordkeeping has to become a habit. Through the years, the persistence of my wife, who has an accounting degree, and my family CPA, has caused me to become a receipt fanatic. I keep *every* receipt on *every* purchase. If you have ever wondered where all the money goes, this is the only way you will ever know. There is a designated place in my wallet where I placed today's receipts: a receipt from the gasoline pump, a receipt from the breakfast meal with my CBMC prayer partners, a receipt for the doughnuts for the office staff, the lunch receipt with one of the investment advisers, a receipt from the car wash, the dry cleaners receipt, the nutrition store receipt, the home improvement store receipt, and if it's my night to cook, the receipt for the wholesale club's rotisserie chicken or the sushi restaurant's take-out. So, if you want to know where all your money is going, or if you want to get all the possible tax deductions for your business to which you are rightfully entitled, start with the receipts. Then, when you reconcile your records and checkbook, it will all make sense.

By the way, this theory also works for weight loss. To get back to my college weight, I had to make one major adjustment. I had to track every calorie that went into my mouth. I then had to reduce the caloric intake for my height and weight to the appropriate calorie budget. It is amazing how you can accomplish a goal through the conscious awareness that only comes by recordkeeping.

Your Emergency Fund

> "A bargain is something you can't use at a price you
> can't resist." – *Franklin Jones*

Life will continuously have its little emergencies. At times those emergencies will be larger than expected. Do you remember when you were first trying to get started financially? You would save a little cash, let's say $914. Then, the car would break, and guess how much the repair bill would be? You guessed it: $914. You would think, "How did it know?" Thankfully, through budgeting, your emergency fund will eventually outgrow your emergencies.

I recommend that you maintain at least three to six months of your expenses in a readily available, check-writing money market account. It's not cash but cash equivalents. If your other investment holdings are not readily marketable (easily liquidated without penalty), then you should boost the emergency fund even more. The key is to have readily available financial resources when faced with the unexpected. This account is not to be spent on your daily living expenses. Those expenses are part of your monthly budget from your regular checking account. This emergency money market account is for emergencies. (Oh yeah, ladies, new shoes are not considered an emergency. Now, a new fishing rod...that's a different story.) JUST KIDDING!

The Rule of 72

The rule of 72, even though not precise to the penny, serves as a great tool to help us understand compound interest. If you take the number 72 and divide it by an assumed interest rate, the answer will be the approximate number of years it will take for that money to double. For instance, if you divide 72 by 3, you get 24. Therefore, money growing at an assumed 3% interest rate will double in approximately 24 years. If you divide 72 by 6, you get 12. Therefore, money growing at an assumed interest rate of 6% will double in approximately 12 years. However, because of compounding, the numbers do not work like many would think. Just because your funds grow at twice the interest rate does not mean you will have twice the money. Compounding means you will have much more than twice as much. Look at the chart below and examine the difference in the growth of $10,000 at 3%, 6% and 12%.

Years	3%	6%	12%
0	$10,000	$10,000	$10,000
6			$20,000
12		$20,000	$40,000
18			$80,000
24	$20,000	$40,000	$160,000
30			$320,000
36		$80,000	$640,000
42			$1,280,000
48	$40,000	$160,000	$2,560,000

Chapter Five

Discipline Five: Retirement Planning

"Life should not be a journey to the grave with the intention of arriving safely in a pretty and well preserved body, but rather to skid in broadside, in a cloud of smoke, thoroughly used up, totally worn out, and loudly proclaiming, 'Wow! What a ride'!"   ---Hunter S. Thompson

A definition of retirement: *You get up in the morning with nothing to do and go to bed at night having only done half of it.*

I once heard of a guy that was diagnosed with A.A.A.D.D. or Age Activated Attention Deficit Disorder. I have also discovered that seniors have their own senior texting codes.

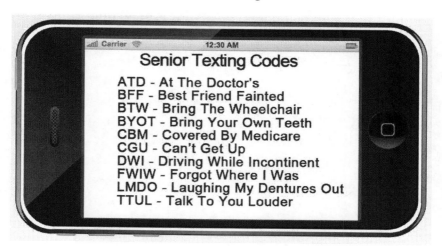

Retirement or Re-engagement?

An interesting difference in the "builder" generation and the "baby boomer" generation is their perspective on retirement. Both generations worked extremely hard in preparation for the day of transition. However, boomers seem to be resisting retirement. Instead they embrace re-engagement. One reason might be that the old pension plans that guaranteed an eventual steady retirement income stream have all but gone by the wayside. The future of social security retirement benefits has become less certain.

Retirement planning is primarily twofold. It addresses the *accumulation phase* and the *income phase* of our financial lives. It is critical to have a laser focus on retirement planning. That focus will mean you have established a *target monthly accumulation goal* as part of your budget. You will then be able to attain your *target retirement nest egg goal* through consistent systematic investing.

Building Wealth: The Accumulation Phase

The Accumulation Phase is the disciplined, systematic investing of assets, primarily throughout the employment years, for the purpose of creating retirement income. The sooner you start saving and accumulating for the future, the sooner you will be able to accomplish your financial goals. *It is amazing how many people have no conscious awareness of a retirement goal and, worse yet, no plan to get there.* Ira

Hayes, a manager in the advertising department of NCR Corporation, once said, "Nothing can be accomplished until you begin. Success is much more quickly attained when you expect it." If you will determine a specific amount of monthly income that you would like coming in at retirement, then your advisor can interpolate the inflation-adjusted *target retirement nest egg goal*. This is a very important number. Once that retirement nest egg goal is determined, the advisor can calculate the amount you need to be systematically investing each month, the *target monthly accumulation goal*. This is a critically important financial number that you must work into your monthly budget. Let me say this as bluntly as I can: If this number does not become part of your monthly lifestyle budget, you will most often come up short at retirement.

Pay Yourself First

If you try to pay all your expenses each month and then save what's left, there will *never* be anything left. Therefore, you must pay yourself first. Your future is your most important creditor. Every month, with no exception, you should place your monthly accumulation amount (let's suppose no less than 10% of your income) away for retirement. You will be amazed at how that amount will build through your relentless discipline. You will also take advantage of an often overlooked financial principle called dollar cost averaging.

Dollar Cost Averaging

Dollar Cost Averaging is an investment strategy in which the investor makes regular periodic deposits over specific time periods into a certain investment. When the price of shares falls, more shares will be purchased because the same dollar amount is being invested, let's say, monthly. When the share price rises, fewer shares will be purchased. The key is that the investment's volatility creates a lower total average cost per share of the investment, giving the investor a lower overall cost for the shares purchased over time.

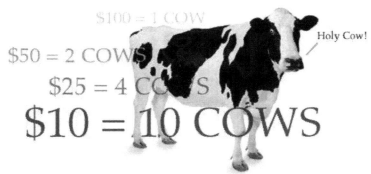

I was conducting an investment training class one day for advisors, and one of my rural Oklahoma advisors spoke up and said, "I can explain Dollar Cost Averaging in a way that people can understand." I said "Okay, Windle, let's hear it." He stood up, began to write on the front board and said, "Let's suppose that a rancher decides to build a herd of cattle. He commits $1000 per month over the next six months to building the herd. In month one cattle cost $1000 per head, so he buys 1 cow. In month two the price of cows falls to

$500, so his $1000 buys 2 cows. In month three the price per head falls to $250, so his $1000 buys 4 cows. In month four the unthinkable happens and the price per head falls to $100, so his $1000 buys 10 cows. Finally, in month five the price per head turns back up to $250, and he buys 4 cows. Then, in month six, the price moves back up to $500 (half the price at which he first started buying), and the rancher buys two cows. He then decides to sell all of the cows. He invested $1000 for six months for a total of $6000. Over that six months, he bought a total of 23 cows and then sells them all at $500 per head for a total sales price of $11,500.

Dollar Cost Averaging and Building a Herd of Cattle

Month Purchased	Amount Invested	Price per Cow	Number
1	$1000	$1000	1
2	$1000	$500	2
3	$1000	$250	4
4	$1000	$100	10
5	$1000	$250	4
6	$1000	$500	2

Total Investment: $6000

Sell All @ $500 each   23 x $500 = **$11,500**

Since that day years ago, I have foregone my fancy financial explanations of Dollar Cost Averaging. Instead, I have told people about Windle's rancher building a herd of cattle. Sometimes simple common sense communicates more effectively than complex financial jargon. Now, take that principle and boldly invest your monthly accumulation amount toward your target retirement nest egg goal.

Should I Contribute to My Company 401(k) Plan?

Anytime a company offers to match the contributions that you voluntarily make into your own retirement plan, you would have to be **CRAZY** not to accept it.

Clueless as to the fact that matching funds are really free.

Ridiculously skeptical that the plan has hidden drawbacks.

Afraid for no reason, their contributions are not vested.

Zero understanding of how dollar cost averaging works.

You can pay yourself first through payroll deductions.

I stood in front of a corporate meeting one day, speaking to a group of employees that were considering participation in their firm's 401(k) plan. I was searching for a way to make the point that they would have to be CRAZY not to participate. You can't call people crazy. That does not go over well. So I simply asked this question: "Does anyone in the room have a five dollar bill?" Reluctantly, they all looked around at one another until, finally, a lady dug in her purse, pulled out her wallet and produced a five dollar bill. I asked," Would you please bring that to me?" She walked to the front of the room and handed me the five. Immediately, I pulled out my wallet, took a five dollar bill, put it with hers and handed her the $10. I said, "Thank you, you may return to your seat." Then I proclaimed to the group, "That is how your matching funds 401(k) plan works." Any questions? Just for the fun of it I asked again, "Now, who else has a five dollar bill?" All hands went up. I said, "Sorry, guys, you'll have to let the company match yours." One lady doubled her money that day. The illustration cost me five bucks, but it was well worth the impact and clarification it brought to the group.

The contributions that you make to your company's 401(k) plan are always vested from day one. That is your money. It will always be your money. The matching funds that your company places into your plan will also be yours, depending on your firm's vesting schedule. For instance, some plans vest over a five year period, 20% each year, until the end of year five, so the matching funds portion is also yours incrementally. The vesting schedule is often 20% year-end one, 40% year-end two, 60% year-end three, 80% year-end four and 100% year-end five. Check with your human resources department and examine your specific plan for the details.

Some of the millionaire clients our firms have assisted with retirement rollovers simply disciplined themselves and maximized their contributions to their company retirement plans. These people are often unassuming, live conservatively and are rarely lavish in their expenditures. They deliberately live below their means. The convenience of payroll deductions helps them pay themselves first. They took advantage of the power of dollar cost averaging and the magic of compound interest. Many of them told me one of the benefits of their participation in their corporate plan is the "out of sight, out of mind" principle. They knew that the payroll deductions would keep their retirement proceeds "out of sight" and therefore keep them from spending their future nest eggs.

Living off Your Nest Egg: The Income Phase

Now that you've accumulated it, let's talk about living off of it. The Income Phase is the disciplined systematic disbursement of assets, as retirement income, with an emphasis on capital preservation. As I have referenced, many families accomplish their *target retirement nest egg goals* through their corporate retirement plans. Others arrive at their goals through their IRA accounts, receiving an inheritance, selling a business, or through a strong personal discipline in accumulating nonqualified (non-retirement) investments. J. Paul Getty is quoted as saying,

"Formula for success: rise early, work hard, strike oil." I would not necessarily count on that...or the lottery. At this point, let's assume it is not important how you arrived at your target retirement nest egg goal as long as you have arrived. The disciplined systematic disbursement of your retirement portfolio throughout the remainder of your life is just as critically important as its accumulation. Since the old pension plans are mostly a thing of the past and the future of Social Security income is questionable, your future income stream will be dependent on your personal investment accumulations.

Capital preservation (protecting your portfolio) now becomes a more important issue than ever before. Risk reduction should be given strong consideration. You no longer have the years to make up for major market declines. I will discuss the damage of the *drawdown effect* in Chapter 7 when we examine Asset Allocation.

There is also a budgeting process that takes place even throughout our retirement income years. Let's call it the **RDB retirement distribution budget**. Investment experts agree that you should attempt to never distribute more than 4% of your retirement portfolio annually. When you first retire, you may think your **target retirement nest egg goal** looks rather large; however, when you realize that you should only be withdrawing 4% of that accumulated value on an annual basis, you gain a new perspective. For instance, if an individual had $1 million accumulated, the 4% annual distribution would be $40,000. Some investors choose to assume the risk of withdrawing larger percentages, and some investors choose to assume the risk of investing more aggressively. Your advisor will also be able to calculate an *inflation adjusted life expectancy distribution*. In this scenario, the investor realizes that he will invade the principle throughout his life expectancy without concern to the eventual distribution of an estate to the next generation.

In determining your *RDB retirement distribution budget*, it is first important to total your retirement income sources. You then examine your total monthly expenditures. As long as your income sources are exceeding your expenditures, you are functioning within your retirement budget. If the monthly expenditures are exceeding your income sources, you will begin exhausting your nest egg. Through the years I've had families say to me, as they have exceeded their *retirement distribution budget*, "Well, we have had a few emergencies." Legitimate emergencies do arise. However, I have also seen emergency cruises, emergency boats, emergency new pickup trucks, emergency campers, and one lady had the best one yet, emergency shoes. Since it's not the advisor's role to tell you how to spend your money, I said, "Ooooh girl, I totally get it."

Honey, I'm Home Forever

In the introduction I mentioned that after one man retired and sat around the house a while, his wife said to me, "Help, my husband has just retired and doesn't know what to do with himself." She continued, "I just realized I now have twice the husband and half the money." Interestingly, some people retire and love every minute of it. Others retire and realize almost immediately that retirement for them was a highly overrated proposition. If you have no hobby, no recreational activity, no ministry or volunteer interests, then you might reconsider whether or not retirement is really for you. Over the years, I have helped many clients transition to retirement. I have seen some retirees that seemed to lose their purpose in life and die within six months after retiring. It was as if life without purpose was not worth living. You must maintain a sense of purpose. Those that wake up every day with purpose are the most inspiring and fulfilled people I know. For instance, one of my retired pastors, well up in his 80s, sat at my conference table, rocking back-and-forth and almost seemed anxious. I called him by name and asked, "Are you doing okay?" He said, "Yes, John. I just wish I had a pulpit to preach in Sunday." Wow, talk about a purpose driven life. He lived every day with a passion to tell people about Jesus Christ. I probed into the reason he lived with such a passion and found a passage in Romans 11:29 that said, "The gifts and the calling of God are irrevocable." In other words, we take our calling, purpose and passion with us to the grave. My own father, now in his mid-80s, even though he said he retired as a pastor 20 years ago, is still engaged in an associate pastoral staff position at his church. I have never known a more fulfilled, passionate human being.

I called my dad recently and asked, "Dad, what are you doing?" With an incredible burst of excitement, he said, "John, I'm reading a book on leadership." You go, Daddy! I have been a blessed son and joyful recipient of many hours of his wisdom, ministry and even the leadership books that he would read and pass on to me.

I recently flew to Georgia to his 85th Birthday celebration. I had a great weekend eating fried catfish and roasted peanuts. I had filed a flight plan for an early departure Monday morning, but when I awoke rainy weather had moved in and there was only a 300 foot ceiling. Since that is below my minimums required for departure I stayed a while longer with my parents. I was privileged to sit in on their devotional time that morning. Later that day I sent out the following text to all the family. One of my nieces replied that it was her favorite text ever and posted it on Facebook.

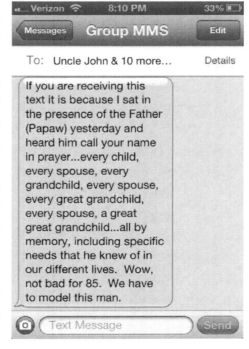

There are so many powerful things that you can continue to do throughout your retirement years to maintain your purpose. Giving of yourself to charitable and spiritual causes seems to be at the top of the list for the those that are the most fulfilled.

Getting All the Life You Can out of the Money You Have

Fulfillment in life and the size of your retirement portfolio are not necessarily correlated. I have known people that are fulfilled and broke, and I have known people that are fulfilled and wealthy. I have known people that are miserable and broke, and I have known people that are miserable and wealthy. Fulfillment has a lot more to do with knowing who you are and where you are going. Try as you may, you really cannot separate the financial, physical, family and spiritual aspects of your life. If you neglect one or more of the four, you cannot expect to be totally fulfilled. For instance, health is wealth. Even though a person may have attained financial and even spiritual soundness, if he chose to live bellied up to the buffet, consuming chicken fried steak and gravy, that will eventually cost him in regards to his physical health. Conversely, if a person immerses himself in physical fitness at the gym or participating in and watching sports, while neglecting his family, financial, or spiritual life, it can eventually take its toll. Balance and moderation help us to live fulfilled and stable lives.

Getting all the life you can out of the money you have requires a deliberate effort on your part to live a well-rounded life. We must take care of ourselves physically, spiritually and emotionally in order to enjoy the financial fruits of our years of labor. What good is it to get to retirement and be a physical, spiritual or emotional mess. Broken people are not always financially broke. Our personal disciplines will shape our physical, financial and spiritual wholeness and impact our fulfillment. *You are the Chief Executive Officer of your personal disciplines*.

We Are Going to Travel When the Dog Dies

I told my wife recently, "We are going to travel when the dog dies." As dog lovers, we both laughed because every time a dog has died in our family, we go out and get another one. That probably means we will eventually die before the dog dies. Oh well. It illustrates the alluring, yet elusive, thoughts we all have about a day we all call "someday." As opposed to waiting until someday, or even trying to outlive the dog, why not put your travel schedule on your calendar today? Even if some of the trips are being planned long in advance, I can assure you that they will not happen without being scheduled. In doing so, my wife and I discovered that not every trip has to be an elaborate out-of-country or even out-of-state trip. There are some awesome extended weekend or even day trips that you can make. A day trip allows you to sleep in your own bed but still visit an amazing site within driving distance. Something refreshing and rejuvenating happens inside you. It is like a breath of fresh air. If you are married or in a relationship, it can even add an invigorating touch. So, get off the sofa, examine your retirement distribution budget and tackle your bucket list. Bucket lists are not just for seniors or terminally ill people. (We are all terminal!) They are for anyone looking to "get all the life he can out of the money he has."

Chapter Six

Discipline Six: Tax Strategies

"I have never met anyone who wakes up on April 15 of each year and joyfully exclaims, 'Oh boy, today I get to pay my taxes!'"   ---John Gillespie

Sometimes I miss the fun quotes from our late, great President Ronald Reagan. He was once quoted as saying, *"The most terrifying words in the English language are: I am from the government and I am here to help."* He is also credited for once saying, *"Government's view of the economy could be summed up in a few short phrases: If it moves, tax it. If it keeps moving, regulate it. If it stops moving, subsidize it."* So today we are faced with an interesting mix of Wall Street and Washington. Only the future will reveal how well the two will get along.

Understanding certain tax strategies can help you to preserve your annual income, minimize the negative tax effect on your total net worth and maximize your eventual gross estate distribution.   There are tax strategies that address the process of tax deferrals, tax exemptions and even tax-free distributions.

Tax deferrals allow investment earnings such as interest, dividends or capital gains to be deferred until the investor withdraws and takes possession of them. The most common types of tax-deferred investments include those in individual retirement accounts (IRAs) and deferred annuities. Instead of paying tax on the returns of an investment, tax is paid only at a later date, leaving the investment to grow unhindered. Investments are usually made when a person is earning higher income and is taxed at a higher tax rate. Withdrawals are often made from an investment account when a person is earning little or no income and can then be taxed at a lower rate.

Tax exemptions are free from, or not subject to, taxation by regulators or government entities. A tax exempt entity can be excused from certain taxation laws. Governments can be trying to encourage investors to invest when exempting taxation. Certain securities or investor groups can be referred to as tax exempt. For example, the interest earned from municipal bonds is exempt from federal or state taxation.

Other forms of tax exempt entities include, but are not limited to, churches, religious organizations, amateur sports leagues and charities that try to provide relief to the poor and underprivileged.

Tax free distributions refer to the distributions from certain types of financial products (such as municipal bonds) that are not taxed and whose earnings are not taxed. The tax free status of these assets may incentivize individuals and businesses to increase spending or investing, resulting in economic stimulus. Governments will often provide a tax break to investors purchasing government bonds to ensure that sufficient funding will be available for expenditure projects.

Filing Your Taxes Is Not the Same as Implementing Tax Strategies

Your expectations of your CPA or tax preparer might very well be unreasonably exaggerated. That person's role is not necessarily to help you save on taxes. Their role is primarily to help you file your taxes. Your expectations should be centered more on timeliness and accuracy. However, your tax preparer cannot read your mind and can only work with the tax information you bring him. Create a *Tax Information File* and be diligent in retaining all W-2s, 1099s, K-1's, year-end investment statements, year-end bank statements, charitable donation receipts, etc. Even if you do not understand it, if it is marked "Tax Information Enclosed," place it in your tax file and take it to your accountant. Preparation prior to your visit with the accountant is critical. It helps to avoid wasting both your time and their time.

Tax Filing Checklist

Step 1: Gather your documents.

- **W-2s** for each job held during the year for each person in the household (this form reports your name, wages, and other tax information to the IRS)
- **1099s** and **1098s** showing other income (unemployment, social security, school loans, health care reimbursement, state tax refund, gambling winnings, contract work) that is reported to the IRS
- **Income/interest statements** received for any savings account/investments
- **Bank account numbers** in the form of voided checks or your bank or credit union's routing number and savings or checking account number are necessary for your refund to be deposited automatically into your account through direct deposit
- **Last year's tax return** (if you have it)

Step 2: Collect information for everyone in your household.

- **Name** and **taxpayer number** as they appear on the Social Security Card (SSN) or Individual Taxpayer Identification Number letter (ITIN) for you and all dependents (including children and elderly relatives for whom you provide care)
- **Date of birth** and **relationship** (son, daughter, mother, etc.)
- **Current address** (may be different from the address on your employment records)

Step 3: Gather additional items to receive a larger refund.

- **Childcare expenses**: name, address, Tax ID or Social Security Number of the child care provider
- **Business expenses and assets**: if you're self-employed or have a small business
- **College**: loans and/or scholarships received, and bills for technical/community college or university (Forms 1098-T/1098-E)
- **Educator expenses** for teaching grades K-12 (school supplies and materials used in the classroom)
- **Charitable donations**: list of contributions and amounts, receipts for contributions
- **Vehicles**: vehicle sales tax, personal property tax statement for each car you own, total miles driven for the year and/or total miles driven for business
- **Renters**: amount of rent paid (in some states)
- **Homeowners**: mortgage interest statement (Form 1098), real estate taxes paid, Statement of Property Tax Payable for the year
- **Retirement/IRA**: amount contributed to an IRA and total value as of December 31
- **ITIN**: if you need to apply for an <u>ITIN</u> for yourself or a family member

IRS Does Not Mean *Ignorant Refund System*

I have never met anyone who wakes up on April 15 of each year and joyfully exclaims, "Oh boy, today I get to pay my taxes." None of us enjoy shelling out our hard earned money to the government. Even though you might or might not agree with certain administrations or political parties, you must admit that our nation's overall infrastructure shines brightly on a global scale. There are good reasons to pay a few taxes.

I prefer driving on paved streets and highways, not dirt roads.

I prefer knowing that law enforcement is in place to protect our communities rather than a world where thugs rummage and pillage at will.

I prefer knowing the fire department will arrive at a crisis rather than having to make do on my own.

I prefer knowing the TSA is screening the passenger next to me rather than watching him detonate his underwear and blowing up the airplane. (Who would have thought such?)

I preferred having our nation protected by a strong military, not one that's underfunded and outdated. (OK, so I got on a soap box!)

The list goes on and on, proving that IRS Internal Revenue Service does not mean ignorant refund system. There is one element, however, that is totally ignorant: the complexity of it all. The Internal Revenue Code (IRC) is ridiculously complex. Until the day we can get a group of politicians to work together toward simplification of the code, we will remain desperately entangled in a web of ridiculous unreasonable rules. The greatest man that ever lived was once asked if it was lawful to pay taxes to the government. Jesus replied by saying, "Render to Caesar the things that are Caesar's, and to God the things that are God's." The biggest problem a nation will ever face is when the government begins to dictate to its people laws that violate God's laws. There are only 10 of them. Look them up in Exodus 20.

The Goal Is Tax Avoidance, Not Tax Evasion

After about 10 Years in the financial services industry, in approximately 1992, I flew into Reno, Nevada to what I thought was going to be an advanced estate planning conference. This was an invitation-only gathering for advanced strategists to discuss tax and estate planning strategies that could be utilized for the benefit of our clients. I soon discovered why the environment seemed to be peculiarly secretive. The meeting lodge was positioned right up against the base of a mountain. There were only about 25 of us in attendance. The coordinators asked for each one of us to introduce ourselves and to briefly tell about our experience in the industry. One by one I began listening to the attendees introduce themselves. As each introduction progressed, the hair began to stand up on the back of my neck. I soon realized that I was the only person in the room who had not either been arrested, served time in prison or was battling a lawsuit over tax issues. Wow! It did not take long for me to realize that I did not want to venture any further down that path. I flew back to Oklahoma City and in-flight wrote out my resignation to the organization that encouraged me to attend that event. Make no mistake: I am a wholehearted believer in tax avoidance. However, I am not a believer in tax evasion. In public speaking engagements, I often jokingly say, "The difference between tax avoidance and tax evasion is 10 to 20 years in the federal penitentiary." *Legitimate tax avoidance strategies utilize the Internal Revenue Code and seek to minimize negative tax impact. You should take advantage of every possible viable tax avoidance strategy that is applicable to you through the code.* For some reason many people seem discontent with mainstream middle-of-the-road tax avoidance strategies. My concern would be that if you get too close to the edge, you might fall off. Years ago, I discussed what sounded like an overly aggressive strategy with my CPA. He said, "John, you can go down that path if you choose and it might work, but you could end up having to fight the IRS for the remainder of your career." I took heed to his advice. He was saying, take advantage of the code, but temper your creative exuberance. Through the years I have watched advisor friends and their clients get too close to the edge. You will want to avoid the financial and time-consuming consequences and hassles that they eventually faced.

Tax Planning Tools

There are many different basic and more advanced tax planning tools. There are even charitable estate planning tools that also have tax benefits. Since various aspects, like maximum contribution limits, can vary annually, I will simply give you a list of some tools for your consideration. Just because it is on the list does not mean you can or even should be utilizing it as a tool in your plan. Be sure to discuss with your advisers the current parameters, personal applicability and tax implications surrounding each of the following:

Retirement Rollovers	IRAs
Certificates of Deposits	Traditional IRAs
Money Market Accounts	Simple IRAs
Mutual Funds	Roth IRAs
Municipal Bond Funds	SEP/IRAs
Universal Life Insurance	401(k) and Solo 401(k)
Variable Life Insurance	403(b)/TSA
Term Life Insurance	Keogh
Variable Annuities	Profit-Sharing Plans
Fixed and Fixed-Indexed Annuities	529 Plans
1031 and 1035 Exchanges	Stretch or Inherited IRAs

Your advisers should also help you take into consideration issues like Early Withdrawal Penalties and RMDs, Required Minimum Distributions. In addressing the ridiculous complexity of it all, think about in this manner: ***There can be tax consequences if you take your money out of certain types of accounts too early, too late, too much or too little.*** See, that's not complicated, now, is it?

Charitable Gifting Strategies

Man cannot journey from survival to success and ultimately from success to significance without examining the philanthropic impact of his life. A greater fear than extinction is extinction without significance. I have found much joy in helping individuals, ministries and other charitable organizations develop stewardship, planned giving and estate planning strategies. This falls under my "what's going to matter 100 years from now" category. Donors can direct gifts of cash, securities, real estate and other assets to charitable organizations while also receiving many estate enhancement benefits. These advanced planning strategies can

- increase your retirement income,

- reduce your capital gains and income tax liability,

- increase your charitable income tax deductions, and

- reduce your estate and inheritance tax liability.

Charitable gifting strategies, in addition to their tax advantages, will most importantly help you to accomplish stewardship and philanthropic fulfillment. These stewardship strategies can help you best utilize the resources given to you and enable you to leave behind an on-going legacy.

Gifts of Cash and Non-Cash Gifts - You gift cash or personal or real property to a qualified charity.

Revocable Living Trusts - You name a qualified charity as one of the beneficiaries of your trust.

Deferred Gift Annuities - You gift assets to a qualified charity in return for an income to be paid to you at some later date.

Immediate Gift Annuities - You gift assets to a qualified charity in return for an income paid to you immediately.

Charitable Remainder Trusts (CRT) - You gift assets to the trust and receive income; charity gets the principle (a.k.a. the "remainder") on your death.

Charitable Lead Trusts (CLT) - You gift assets to the trust; charity receives income over your lifetime or trust period. Afterward, assets are distributed as you designate.

Gifts of Life Insurance - You name a qualified charity as the owner and beneficiary of an insurance policy.

Pay on Death (POD) Designation - You authorize a bank or financial institution to pay the balance of your account to a qualified charity.

Life Estate - You gift real estate but retain its use and control.

Loss Sell and Gift - You sell an asset for less than fair market value and contribute the proceeds to a qualified charity.

The impact you can have in the lives of others through charitable gifting brings an indescribable sense of fulfillment. Knowing that you have changed someone's life for the better is an awesome thing. We were not placed here just to make a living. We were placed here to make a difference. Winston Churchill once said, "You make a living by what you get, you make a life by what you give".

Chapter Seven

Discipline Seven: Asset Allocation

"When a person with money meets a person with experience, the person with the experience winds up with the money and the person with the money winds up with the experience."
---Harvey MacKay

Asset Allocation is an investment strategy that aims to balance risk and reward by apportioning a portion of a portfolio's assets according to an individual's time horizon, risk tolerance and investment objectives. This is not an issue of one person being right and another being wrong. This is an issue of personal comfort and suitability.

Time Horizon takes into consideration both the number of years you have to accumulate assets and the number of years you will need to take income from those accumulated assets once you retire. To play it safe, you should think beyond your life expectancy years.

Risk Tolerance is typically measured during a discovery interview with your advisor through a risk profile questionnaire. If your profile reveals that you are *risk tolerant,* then it is translated to mean you are willing to accept and deal with risks. If your profile reveals that you are *risk adverse,* then it is translated to mean you desire to remove or transfer risk. If your profile reveals that you are *risk neutral,* you will analyze and seek to mitigate risks as conditions demand.

Investment Objectives deal with your goals for a specific portfolio. If goals change over the years, you will want to keep your advisor informed as to such changes. It is important for your advisor to know what you are wanting to accomplish with your various investment accounts.

There are typically three main assets classes – equities, fixed income, and cash and equivalents. Each has different levels of risk and returns so each will behave differently over time. All three main asset classes might or might not be appropriate within your personal portfolio.

Active vs. Static Allocation and the Drawdown Effect

The real question that investors face in this technically advanced global investing environment is "Will your portfolio be actively managed or statically managed?" In other words, will funds be moved in and out of the market based on certain market indicators, or will you continue to be a buy-and-hold investor? In recent days I have wanted to ask investors, "Do you believe in buy and hold? How's that working for you?" One reason it is so important to embrace active management is to seek to minimize the drawdown effect within a portfolio. *Drawdown effect* means this: if you lose ten percent of your holdings, it does not take ten percent to get back to where you were; it takes eleven percent. If you lose 20%, it takes 25% gain just to gain it back. If you lose 30%, it takes 43% to gain it back. Here is an easy one to understand: if a person had $500,000 but lost 50% of it, he now only has $250,000. In order to get back to $500,000, it will take a 100% return on the $250,000 to simply break even. The numbers do not work the way you would normally think.

Drawdown Effect

% Loss	% Gain Required
10%	11%
20%	25%
30%	43%
40%	67%
50%	100%
60%	150%
70%	233%
80%	400%
90%	900%
100%	Broke

Fundamental, Strategic, and Technical Analysis

Various types of analysis will surge to investment headlines from time to time. We believe a prudent approach to active asset allocation should include all three types of analysis.

First, **fundamental analysis** can basically tell an advisor "what to buy." Fundamental analysis will evaluate a security by attempting to measure its intrinsic value by examining related economic and financial factors. A fundamentalist will attempt to study everything that can affect a security's value, including macroeconomic factors (like the overall economy and industry conditions) and individually specific factors (like the financial condition and management of companies). Fundamentals are an important factor.

Secondly, **strategic analysis**, can tell an advisor how much of an asset class or a security to buy. Strategic analysis can involve periodically rebalancing the portfolio in order to maintain a long term goal for asset allocation. At the inception of the portfolio, a "base asset mix" is established based on expected returns. Because the value of assets can change given market conditions, the portfolio constantly needs to be readjusted to meet the specified mix. Strategic analysis can assist the investor in the avoidance of becoming over-weighted or under-weighted in an asset class or specific security.

Thirdly, **technical analysis** can assist an advisor in knowing when to buy or when to sell. Technical analysis is a method of evaluating securities by analyzing statistics generated by market activity such as past prices and volume. Technical analysts do not attempt to measure a security's intrinsic value but instead use charts and other tools to identify patterns that can suggest future activity. Technical analysts believe that historical performance of stocks and markets can be indications of future performance. These analysts are often referred to as chartists. Chart patterns have specific meanings. One challenge that investors face is to find a true chartist who has become skilled in his craft. Maybe this analogy can help. In a shopping mall, a fundamental analyst would go to each store, study the product being sold and then decide whether to buy it or not. By contrast, a technical analyst would sit on a bench in the mall and watch people going into the stores. Disregarding the intrinsic value of the products in the store, his or her decision would be based on the patterns or activity of people going into each store. Technical analysts monitor daily market indicators. It is really simple: *you either believe in buy and hold or you believe there are times to be in the market and times to be out.*

The Investment Markets Meltdown

For the first 18 years of my now over 30 years in the investment industry, I believed in buy and hold. However, when the technology bubble busted in the spring of 2000 and I began to watch the markets unravel, I knew there had to be a better way to manage money. I knew I needed some visual mechanism that could help me protect my clients' money. I began studying everything I could find about technical analysis. Unlike the traditional industry conferences that I had attended for years, there were times I would fly in to a technical analysis investment conference to discover I was the only "industry" person there. Everyone else would be "traders," sharpening their charting skills.

Knowing there is no crystal ball, and knowing you will never catch the exact top or the exact bottom, a skilled chartist will have specific signals that will trigger him to take positions and sell positions. In the beginning, I would only use fundamental and strategic analysis to determine a client portfolio allocation. We would then hold on to whatever we had purchased, and I would tell the client what the industry had taught me to say:

- Buy and hold, and over time everything will just work out. (Do most people really have 30 years between the kids' college years and their retirement?)
- Just hold on…it's probably going to be a small correction.

- But, if you sell now, you're locking in a loss.
- If you missed the best 10 days of the last 30 years...
- We've got to be getting close to the bottom
- If you'll just diversify across these 9 style boxes, ...

I now classify all of the above as "Believable Misinformation." The problem with these statements is that at times they can be partially true. *It is the cyclical and repetitive market meltdowns that can eventually take away your retirement. Your advisor must be utilizing some tactical active management process for the protection of your portfolio.* Why does the industry teach advisors to say all of this "believable misinformation" stuff? The answer is simple: money. Think about it from their perspective. No matter what investment fund group you are using, they all have built-in expense ratios, even "No load" funds. Their equity funds, understandably, carry higher expense ratios than their money market fund. Therefore, if you leave their equity fund and go to their money market account to wait out a market storm, they are losing money. So the only choice they have to keep from losing money is to encourage the advisors to keep their clients fully allocated at all times.

Will It Be Different This Time?

The investment markets can be ruthlessly insensitive at times. If you examine the Dow Jones Industrial Average (DJIA) for the past 100 years, you will notice that for almost 20 years, the DJIA basically ran flat.

Then a tremendous surge took place in the markets we often refer to as the Roaring Twenties. You know what happened in 1929, 1930 and 1931. The Great Depression hit, and the drawdown effect was so severe that literally 25 years later investors were just getting back to where they had been prior to the crash. Interestingly enough, fortunes were actually earned in the years after the Depression by investing in certain sectors, being willing to take profits and then sitting on the sidelines during times of drawdown. During the 50s the baby boomers are credited for creating a new market surge. Those born from 1946 to 1964 still have impact in various industries when studying age wave demographics. Then, from the mid-60s to the early 1980s, the markets again went almost nowhere. I entered this industry in 1982 and wondered why almost no one wanted to talk about equity investing. From the mid-80s until spring of 2000, there was a phenomenal surge in equity values, and Wall Street had chimpanzees throwing darts at stocks and outperforming advisors. However, did you notice the headlines by March 2009, things like "investors lose 12 years of returns?" Some investors found themselves back at their 1997 values. In 2013 many investors were still just getting back to where they were in 2007. They were also at the same place in 2000. Could it be we have reentered one of those flat times in equity investing or *will it be different this time*? Will we have a breakout or a breakdown? Systems cannot really be predictive, but they absolutely must be reactive. The market's volatility has again caused active asset allocation to become of great interest to many.

Age Wave Demographics and Why Diversification Is Overrated

Age wave demographics tell us that the baby boomers had a significant impact on the baby food industry in the 1950s. As they aged, there was a surge in the toy industry in the 1960s, the fast food industry in the 1970s and eventually clothing, cars, homes, mortgages, and on and on. However, if the peak spending years for an individual aged 46 to 50, then could it be possible that the baby boomers are beginning to surpass their peak spending years? One of the fuels for any economy is family spending. All countries are not affected the same regarding age wave demographics; therefore, global awareness has become a must in the actively-managed diversified portfolio. Could it be that alternative investments, commodities, energy, precious metals should also be considered? Absolutely. However, there are times that diversification is not the answer.

Diversification, in and of itself, is not the end-all answer. Diversification is often overrated. In 2008 all nine of the equity style boxes (large growth, large blend, large value, mid-growth, mid-blend, mid value, small growth, small blend, small value), suffered at least a 30% drawdown. Remember how much you have to gain if you suffer a 30% drawdown? How about 43%?! *There are times that larger concerns like demographic issues and geopolitical concerns weigh more heavily on the markets. There are times a rising tide raises all ships and a lowering tide lowers all ships.*

Active asset allocation will often incorporate momentum investing. Momentum investing is an investment strategy that aims to capitalize on the continuance of existing trends in the market. The momentum investor believes that large increases in the price of a security will be followed by additional gains and vice versa for declining values. The basic idea is that once a trend is established, it is more likely to continue in that direction than to move against the trend. Another technical indicator can be the Relative Strength Index (RSI). RSI is a technical momentum indicator that compares the magnitude of recent gains to recent losses in an attempt to determine over-bought and over-sold conditions of an asset. The list of technical indicators is extensive. The additional work involved to assess the daily market indicators is often more than an advisor can bear. Technology has paved the way to more quickly review market data knowing that someone in Brazil, Russia, India and China is possibly reviewing the same material.

A Quantum Leap in Technical Analysis

Technology has caused a quantum leap in technical analysis. Is it possible that "modern portfolio theory" has become "dated" theory? According to the theory, it is possible to construct "an efficient frontier" of optimal portfolios offering the maximum possible expected return for a given level of risk. This theory was pioneered by Harry Markowitz in his paper *"Portfolio Selection,"* published in 1952 by the Journal of Finance. Do you think a few things have changed in terms of technological advancement since 1952? Look inside the cockpit at the 1952 technology of a T-33 airplane.

1952 T-33 Cockpit

As a private pilot, I flew a 1975 Bellanca Super Viking for ten years. The technology, at that time, was state of the art. In actuality I did not even have GPS for a number of years.

1975 Bellanca Super Viking

Now take a look inside the cockpit of one of the new Cirrus TAAs, technically advanced aircraft.

Cirrus SR-22 G3

The Cirrus SR22 wraps technology around the pilot, greatly increasing situational awareness. I now sit in front of two computer screens, one a primary flight display and the other a multi-flight display with all of the current bells and whistles the mind can comprehend. If all else fails, the pilot or passenger can reach up and pull the CAPS handle (Cirrus Airframe Parachute System). A rocket launcher will blow a parachute though the back fuselage of the aircraft, allowing the entire aircraft to be safely lowered to the ground. Yes, technology has truly changed since 1952. If it makes sense to have an aircraft equipped with a parachute, would it also make sense for your retirement portfolio to have a parachute of its own? There is a debate as to who actually said it, possibly Mark Twain or Will Rogers, but someone once said, "I am more concerned with the return of my money than the return on my money."

Cirrus Airframe Parachute System

Today's financial and economic environment might call for additional safety measures. Technology is more advanced than ever before. Having an advisory team that is willing to learn to use it to your benefit might possibly help to preserve your financial future. When the financial market's engine begins to sputter, as history shows it will from time to time, it will be important to have some procedural parachute system in place to take you safely to the ground. How many more market crashes can your portfolio endure?

Rebalancing Is Not Active Asset Allocation

Often, investors and even advisors mistake rebalancing with active asset allocation. They also struggle with the inability to convert analysis into action. Rebalancing is not a form of tactical allocation resulting from technical analysis. Rebalancing is only adjusting existing positions back to their initial allocation originated by strategic analysis. Rebalancing actually just sells your winners and buys more of your losers. Of course, that is not always the right thing to do. Rebalancing does not give your winners the opportunity to run, and it can fuel your losers with more money to lose. Just because a portfolio is rebalanced back to an appropriate asset mix does not mean those asset classes might not be on the brink of a major selloff. During the first half of 2008, the energy sector was booming even though most equities were collapsing. However, when energy began to selloff, many sought refuge in the fixed income or bond market. Amazingly, even the bond market began to slip, and at that time, the only safe haven was cash and cash equivalents. Never forget that cash is an asset class. It seems that the investment industry as a whole would rather you forget such.

What Is Your Sell Discipline?

I have had the privilege through the years to train some great investment advisors. I will often say to them, "Let me see if I can describe your buy discipline." I then proceed to explain a blend of fundamental and strategic allocation strategies, dividing the client's assets across the multiple asset classes, possibly including alternative assets and even recommending rebalancing from time to time. Most advisors agree that this sounds appropriate. I didn't ask this question, "Can you explain to me your sell discipline?" It almost never fails. The majority look at me in bewilderment. Some admit that they have no intention of ever leaving the markets. Some even adamantly exclaim, "You can't time the market!" I then realize they have no sell discipline. Furthermore, they have no system that will get their clients' out of the market by Thursday if they need to exit. *Active asset allocation is not about timing the market. It is about responding to major market trends when the markets have violated predetermined, meticulously calculated technical indicators.* As diligently as you have worked to accumulate assets, you must have the assurance that there is a protection discipline in place to sweep your investment portfolio to safety during times of cyclical market meltdowns.

Conclusion

You Will Leave a Legacy

Money isn't the most important thing in life, but it's reasonably close to oxygen on the "gotta have it" scale. ---
Zig Ziglar

Seasick Steve recorded and released his third album back in 2008 that contained the title song "**I Started Out with Nothin' and I Still Got Most of It Left.**" If you are a blues fan, like me, it is worth a YouTube listen. Even though that is probably not a legacy you would want to leave, I can assure you that true fulfillment does not come from the size of your temporal earthly asset base. True fulfillment will come more from knowing who you are, knowing whose you are and knowing that your lifelong efforts continue to have positive lasting impact in the lives of others.

You will leave a legacy. The only question is whether or not it will be the one you hope to leave. The Merriam-Webster dictionary defines legacy as something transmitted by or received from an ancestor or predecessor or from the past. For many, their mind immediately goes to money. Your money is only a piece of your legacy. Your money is not your wealth. Your wealth is your journey, your family, your contribution into the lives of others. Your wealth is the impact you are having and will have going forward.

What Really Matters?

Who you are matters much more to your family than *what you are*. After serving all these years as the investment advisor for hundreds of families and assisting many of them through the accumulation, income, distribution and estate settlement process, I can assure you that *the financial inheritance that you leave your heirs will pale in insignificance compared to the life legacy that you leave*. In fact, I have personally watched in amazement as sizable financial inheritances disappear into oblivion shortly after the deaths of both parents. If it is important to you that your heirs not squander away their inheritance, then you must convey a strong value system or structure a spendthrift provision within your estate's distribution. *Wealth rarely lasts a second generation and almost never a third.* It is not because your heirs intend to blow it all. They often have great intentions. The problem lies partly in the fact that they never grasped Chapter 2 of this book, Discipline Two: Cash Management. They do not realize that a large lump sum inheritance does not mean that you can throw the word *budget* out the window. Remember, we talked about the fact that no matter how much it is, without some form of budget, *you can spend it all!*

I recently sat in a family meeting as a pastor friend talked with our family about the legacy my mother-in-law left behind. He was preparing her eulogy for the next day. When I wrote about her in Chapter 3, regarding long-term care coverage, none of us knew that Alzheimer's would take its toll before I completed this book. My brother-in-law shared a story I had never heard. When he was a little boy, each day before he would leave for school, his mother would place her hands on his shoulders and pray aloud for him. One day, in the busyness of the moment, she forgot to pray. Young David just stood there...and stood there. Eventually, his mom realized what he was doing. So she walked over to him, put her hands on his shoulders and prayed. David ran out the door confidently and was off to school. While David retold that story, the entire family wept. Now that's legacy. That really matters.

The Big Picture - Macro Strategic Planning

We all enter the world naked, unable to feed ourselves and totally dependent on others. Even though life takes us all on various financial journeys, we all eventually exit this world, to a great extent, in pretty much the same condition in which we entered it.   Let me give you some questions to ponder. Why not go ahead and write down your answers?

1.   If you could wave a magic wand and create the perfect lifestyle or existence for your family, what would it be like?

2.   If you could throw away your calendar and replace it with one that took full advantage of your time, talent and resources, what would it look like?

3.   If you could change any list of things in the world, your community and your country, what would they be?

4.   How do you feel about your religion?

5.   How do you feel about your heirs?

6.   What would you like to provide for your heirs while you are alive?

7.   What would you like to provide for your heirs after your death?

8.   How do you feel about your spouse?

9.   What is preventing or delaying you from doing those things that are the best use of your time, talent and resources?

10.   Of your existing advisors, list those whose counsel you respect (friends, spouse, professionals, etc.).

11.   Of your existing advisors, who should be included in the decision-making process?

12.   What is the purpose of money?

Your contemplation and responses to the above questions will assist your wealth management coach in aligning your comprehensive plan with your personal values. Total fulfillment in life has more to do with your contribution into the lives of other people than their contribution into yours. A deadly EF5 tornado ripped through the heart of Moore, Oklahoma on May 20, 2013. We all sensed a desire to try to help. In the following days my wife loaded up her certified TDI (Therapy Dogs International) dog, an 11-pound Papillion (little dog, big butterfly ears), and headed into the crisis. If you are simply bringing calm and joy into the lives of others, you are making a contribution.

I once heard of a little girl who was late coming home from school. When her mother inquired as to what had taken so long, the little girl said she had come across her friend Mary, who was crying because she had broken her doll. Her mother responded, "You don't know anything about repairing dolls." "No," the girl said, "I just sat down next to her and helped her cry."

Your Family Vision

Leaders cast vision. Leaders get up every day and work on living their lives in such a manner so that they will have no regrets. Let's examine some common regrets.

- One of the most common regrets comes from the workaholic who later confesses that he wishes he had spent more time with his family and less time at the office.

- Many wish they had embraced what was right, avoided wrong and stood up to bullies.

- Some regret not staying in touch with family and friends.

- Others would have turned off the phone more often.

- Many people wish they had not worried so much about what other people think of them.

- Too often we realize we did not have enough confidence in ourselves.

- Some people wish they had pursued their dreams rather than living out the expectations of their parents.

- Eventually, we might all wish we had laughed more.

- Instead of waiting for the dog to die, in order to travel, why not travel now and take the hairy mutt with you.

- Many regret giving up on their marriage.

- I often meet people who wish they had made peace with family members. (You can do it. Go make that call.)

- Others wish they had never gotten involved with the wrong people.

- Our nation is now filled with those who wish they had taken better care of their health.
- Ultimately, we will all wish we had invested more of our lives in things that result in eternal value. My parents taught us as kids that there

are only two things that truly have lasting value: the Word of God and the soul of man.

The wonderful thing about vision is that, like morning, it enables us to rise up from the dark moments in our lives into new sunlight. *Vision equips us to permanently close the door on past regrets and move forward with our lives.* People, hopes and dreams perish without vision.

My friend Greg Gunn and I worked together in financial services during the first 10 years of my three decade career. A few years ago Greg sold his company and is now the founder of a powerful ministry, Family I.D. (Intentional Direction). He now focuses on building godly generations by helping families strengthen relationships and build *family mission statements*. His motto is "Write It down, Live It out." Greg says that it is not enough to simply write it down and never look at it again. We must continuously revisit our family mission statement.

What do you hold most important in your family. Your family's vision will come from your core values. Your values will guide you to your family goals. Your goals will give you a clear target as you live out your values, develop the skills within each family member to function viably in society, value one another, treat others with kindness and respect and ultimately fulfill your purpose.

Since we still live in a great nation that allows freedom of speech, let me take the opportunity, in the concluding lines of this book, to simply state my personal mission. *My life mission is "to love and honor my wife and children and redistribute the world's wealth for my clients' benefit in a way that glorifies God, maximizes investment return, minimizes taxation and optimizes its philanthropic impact."* That mission, which burns passionately in this businessman's heart, led our family to form the Carved in Stone Foundation in 1999. The foundation's purpose and our family's mission is "to call people to embrace God's value system, the Ten Commandments, and to live transformed lives evidenced by changed behavior."

When All Is Said and Done

Geoff Moore wrote a beautiful song that carries a powerful message. On my father's 80th birthday, the church in which he was pastoring decided to set aside a special appreciation day in his honor. This song was sung during the morning worship service.

"When All Is Said and Done"

When the music fades into the past,

When the days of life are through,

What will be remembered of where I've come?

When all is said and done?

Will they say I loved my family?

That I was a faithful friend?

That I lived to tell of God's own son?

When all is said and done.

Of how I long to see the hour,

When I would hear that trumpet sound.

So I could rise and see my Savior's face,

And see him smile,

And say, 'Well done.'

You can forget my name

And the songs I've sung,

Every rhyme and every tune.

But remember the truth of Jesus' love,

When all is said and done

When all is said and done.

Made in the USA
San Bernardino, CA
10 February 2016